BOLD

A LIFE OF FAITH AND ACTION

Desi,
We appreciate your heart for people and for missions.
Blessings,
Mark
Karen

Mark Anderson

Bold: A Life of Faith and Action

Unless otherwise noted, all Scripture is taken from THE HOLY BIBLE, NEW INTERNATIONAL VERSION®, NIV® Copyright © 1973, 1978, 1984, 2011 by Biblica, Inc.® Used by permission. All rights reserved worldwide.

Scripture marked NKJV taken from the New King James Version®. Copyright © 1982 by Thomas Nelson. Used by permission. All rights reserved.

Scripture marked NCV taken from the New Century Version®. Copyright © 2005 by Thomas Nelson. Used by permission. All rights reserved.

ISBN: 978-0-578-98352-3

Acknowledgements

To Karen, my wife and best friend. You've been my soulmate since we were teenagers. Your godly example as a wife, mother, and partner in ministry has helped shaped what I believed.

To our six children, you are all amazing gifts from God. Your love toward the Lord brings great joy to my life.

To Barb, my assistant, who for many years has dealt with my quirks, offered valuable guidance, and faithfully administered the various ministries.

Special thanks to those who have helped me write, rewrite, and then rewrite again parts of this book. Our daughter Kirsten, Ashley and Jenna who were my PAs for a season, my current PA Mary Gin, and especially my wife Karen who has read these stories more than I have.

Table of Contents

A Prelude: The Young Army 1

Introduction: We Are in a Battle 13

Chapter 1: Becoming a Jesus Freak 17

Chapter 2: God, What am I Doing? 33

Chapter 3: The Test of Faith 47

Chapter 4: Living My Generational Blessing 63

Chapter 5: Being Bold 77

Chapter 6: From Some to All 89

Chapter 7: Radical Faith 101

Chapter 8: Whole Nations 115

Chapter 9: God's Design: Prayer and Missions Together 139

Chapter 10: What Would It Take to Finish the
Great Commission? 145

Chapter 11: Seeing All 155

Chapter 12: Engaging All 163

Forward by Loren Cunningham

I want to commend Mark Anderson to you. I have had the privilege of knowing him for several decades, and I can tell you that I have been inspired by the bold way he seeks to live his life as a follower of Jesus. As you read through this book you will read of the times we have been bold together for the cause of Christ. You can have a part in this ongoing story, for it is still being shaped. In fact, you can have a key part, a transformative part, a bold part.

Therefore, I want to encourage you to read this book with expectancy. Prepare your heart to become like the men of Issachar who "understood the signs of the times and knew the best course" of action to take (1Ch 12:32). Prepare your heart to be inspired. But don't stop there – the stories that you will read about here are real. And they could be your stories too. So prepare your heart to take action, to be bold.

As you read this book you will be inspired to **BELIEVE**. Believe that God can speak to you and believe him when he does. We know that, "without faith it is impossible to please God, because anyone who comes to him must believe that he exists and that he rewards those who earnestly seek him" (Heb 11:6). As you read of how Mark rose up to the faith challenges before him, take heart! This is a time for all the people of God to arise in faith and believe in the great God who does great exploits through ordinary people – through me and you. There is a great journey of bold faith ahead of you. Don't hold back. Pursue God and allow him to lead you in ways that reflect his remarkable character. You will have to swim against the current if you are going to be transformative change-maker. So give it your all. Be bold!

As you read this book you will be inspired to **OBEY**. It is not enough to hear God's word. We must apply it. The Scriptures exhort us: "Love the Lord your God and keep his requirements, his decrees, his laws and his commands always" (Deu 11:1). In the pages that follow, Mark will share what happened as he obeyed God. It flowed from his love for God, and so it must be for you too. Let God be the center of your affection. If you set your heart to know and love him above all else, the natural overflow of that love will express itself in bold, passionate obedience. Jesus said, "Anyone who loves me will obey my teaching" (Joh 14:23). Bold obedience flows from great love. So be bold in love and obedience!

As you read this book you will be called to **LIVE** your whole life fully for God. He's the giver of life and the only one worthy to be followed unreservedly! In Mark's story you will hear the tale of a follower of Jesus who has sought to keep following the Lord in every season of life. Following Jesus is not a passing fad, but a life-long pursuit, with every increasing opportunities to spread the Kingdom of God to the least, the last and the lost. So wherever you are in your journey with God, set your heart to live your whole life for his glory. Just as Samuel was "given over to the Lord" for "his whole life" (1Sa 1:28), so give your whole life to God. And do it boldly!

As you read this book you will be called to **DECIDE** to make God the supreme Lord of your life. Mark will share how his encounters with God led to decisive action. Like Joshua of old this book will press you to "choose today whom you will serve" (Jos 24:15). Or perhaps you will sense an echo of the words of Elisha, "If the Lord is God, follow him!" (1Ki 18:21). It is time to decide. Decide to believe God. Decide to obey his word to you. Decide to live your life fully for him. This is what it means to be BOLD:

- **B**elieve
- **O**bey
- **L**ive
- **D**ecide

Read Mark's book. Be inspired. Read God's Book. Do these four things. And you will become the bold person for the Kingdom that God has called you to be.

Loren D Cunningham
October 1, 2021

A Prelude

The Young Army

The following spiritual encounter really started with my wife Karen in early June of 2008. She was convicted that the Anderson house was "growing dull" spiritually. In particular, she felt I was becoming dull, but being the gracious wife she is, she didn't *tell* me that. Karen knew it would be way more effective to let the Holy Spirit do the talking. So she responded to her conviction with several weeks of fasting and prayer, asking for a fresh encounter for us all.

Karen felt the Lord was trying to talk to me but that I wasn't listening. In my dullness, I wasn't tuned in and was drifting into spiritual complacency. As it turns out, just because you're doing exciting things in missions, it doesn't mean you're necessarily enjoying a vibrant, personal walk with the Lord.

I was traveling up to two hundred days per year. Jet lag had become an almost permanent state of being for my mind and body. Many days, I felt I was living in two different time zones, trying to force my rhythmic body clock back to the central time zone of Kansas City. I was mostly just coasting in my walk with Jesus, existing in something of a survival mode because of my intense travel and work schedule. Looking back, I realized I could have been more intentional in my relationship with the Lord. I could have done more to seek a fresh word or encounter with Him. Instead I chose comfort and watching sports on TV as a way of escape.

Even I was getting a sense I was missing something. I had lost a prophetic understanding of what God was doing on the earth. In the Old Testament, the tribe of Issachar was known for having "men who understood the times and knew what Israel should do" (1 Chronicles 12:32). There was an unseen world of activity, but I was oblivious to it, because I hadn't taken the time to get into God's presence and listen to His voice. I was stuck but didn't know it. I needed to become like the men of Issachar; I needed to understand the times so I could know what to do.

Then one morning, without warning, Karen's prayers were answered. What happened next was unlike anything I had ever experienced before—an intense encounter that lasted for three days, with dreams, open visions, and the internal, audible voice of the Lord. I didn't have to ask God why this was happening; I already knew. It had to do with an assignment. I had the strong sense it was important to God, and it would define much of my future.

I believe this vision is for all of us. We are all part of "The Young Army."

Day 1: August 12, 2008

At 6:30 a.m. on a Tuesday, I was woken up with the words of Isaiah 43:19 exploding in my spirit! It was almost like God was speaking the verse out loud in the room, "See, I am doing a new thing! Now it springs up; do you not perceive it?" I sat up in bed and said, "What, Lord? What is the new thing?"

Though physically shaken, I managed to get out of bed and get dressed as my sense of the Lord's presence increased. Pacing the floor, I began to understand some future events that would be epic in nature and affect the whole earth. *The demonic forces behind the old Soviet Union are not gone and will rise again.* I could see a picture of communism expanding on the global map, affecting Asia, the Middle East, even the African continent.

We had all assumed that the collapse of the Soviet Union, the tearing down of the Berlin Wall in 1989, was the end of that regime. Now I understood the evil principalities and powers hadn't ceased to exist but were going to oppress nations again through different methods. I found myself asking, "But how Lord? And what does this have to do with me?"

Without answering my questions, God brought another revelation. *A new form of radical Islam will rise up in the Middle East, focused on destroying Israel and the Christian church.* I somehow knew this new group would be extraordinarily evil and apocalyptic in spirit, consumed with destroying everything good and innocent.

Seeing the violent, hostile nature of these two forces aligning shook me up. This kind of evil combined with massive resources could change the whole world as we know it.

What disturbed me the most was our blindness in the church in the Western world, not understanding what was coming—an unengaged church without any clear mission, lacking a paradigm of war.

One thing was very clear to me: everything in the world was about to intensify. The ebb and flow of the coming spiritual battle would move very fast. God had just spoken to me about world-shifting events that would dominate the coming season.

I walked over to the computer we had on the desk next to our bed and turned on the 24/7 livestream from the International House of Prayer. I needed this worship in the background to help me pray over what I had just heard.

A few minutes later, an inner voice began to speak to me. "Are you hungry to hear? Do you have eyes to see? I will give you revelation according to your hunger. I want all of your heart. I want to tell you what lies ahead. I know your failures, but if you give yourself fully to Me I will use you even in your weakness."

I found myself saying, "Yes, Lord! I give myself completely to You. Let me hear Your voice. Let me see what You see."

Pacing in the bedroom, I continued to pray in the spirit. Suddenly, Psalm 2 erupted in my heart:

> *Why do the nations conspire*
> *and the peoples plot in vain?*
> *The kings of the earth rise up*
> *and the rulers band together*
> *against the* LORD *and against his anointed, saying,*
> *"Let us break their chains*
> *and throw off their shackles."*
>
> *The One enthroned in heaven laughs;*
> *the Lord scoffs at them.*
> *He rebukes them in his anger*
> *and terrifies them in his wrath, saying,*
> *"I have installed my king*
> *on Zion, my holy mountain."*
>
> *I will proclaim the* LORD*'s decree:*

> *He said to me, "You are my son;*
> *today I have become your father.*
> *Ask me,*
> *and I will make the nations your inheritance,*
> *the ends of the earth your possession. (vv. 1–8)*

The voice of the Lord spoke to my heart, "The nations are Mine. If you obey and follow Me, I will give them to you." I knew this wasn't about power or wealth, but rather an answer to my many prayers asking for the opportunity to advance the kingdom of God in the countries of the world.

I trembled, trying to grasp all that was happening. "I am moving quickly to the battle line. Run with Me," the Lord continued to speak. "I don't show you the nations to frustrate you. I have made you a warrior. You were designed by Me for battle. I made you this way. Stir it up!"

It was now ten o'clock, and I noticed a new worship band coming onto the stage on the IHOP prayer room livestream. I walked over to the computer screen to get a closer look. The prophetic singer, Misty Edwards, was behind the piano. As the camera moved to the left, I saw that the founder of IHOP, Mike Bickle, had moved to a microphone on stage.

As Misty began to play and sing, it was neither soft nor melodic; it sounded more like a call to battle. It seemed to me that her song went with what God was speaking to my heart. As she played, God's presence in the bedroom grew stronger and stronger.

And then Mike spoke: "Behold! I do a new thing; do you perceive it?" It was like he had a script from my encounter in the bedroom. "Are you hungry to hear? Do you have eyes to see? I will give you revelation according to your hunger. I want all of your heart. I want to tell you what lies ahead. I know your failures, but if you give yourself fully to me, I will use you, even in your weakness." Misty sang what Mike had just said several times over. This worship set continued for two hours.

I was stunned by what was happening. I found a notepad and quickly began writing down the whole experience. I didn't want to leave the bedroom in fear that it would stop, but I felt I had to tell Karen. So I shouted from the bedroom door. Karen came up and joined me for the next two hours. I tried to explain what was happening as well as I could. She acted like she had expected all of this. Of course, she had been the one who prayed for a month that revelation would come.

I decided not to leave the room. I worshipped, prayed, and read the Bible through the afternoon. It was early evening when new revelations began to come. I saw three visions, one after another, almost like scenes on a movie set.

In the first scene, I saw a nursing home with residents sitting around in pajamas, listening to old songs, and reminiscing about old times. They didn't seem old enough to be in a nursing home. They were still in their sixties and seventies, but they seemed convinced their best days were behind them.

Suddenly, everything changed. The second scene was a living room with several couches, all facing an old TV. Sitting on the couches were people in their forties and fifties. They were slouched down, moving in and out of sleep. They seemed out of shape, like they hadn't moved in a long time. The coffee table in front of them was filled with junk food. Though the TV was on, the programming had ended, and nobody cared.

Then the scene changed again. I saw a sea of young men and women, too many of them to count. They were dressed as soldiers, like an ancient army ready for battle. Their helmets, vests, tunics, and shoes resembled the attire of Roman soldiers during the time of Christ.

It was an extraordinary supernatural encounter, but I had no way of knowing it would last for three days.

Day 2: August 13, 2008

The supernatural presence of God never lifted. I felt it all night long as I slept and when I woke up the next day, Wednesday, August 13.

I had so many questions for the Lord. What did the three scenes I had seen the day before mean? Why had He shown them to me? I spent the morning in worship and Bible study. It was midday when the three scenes opened up to me again.

I was back in the nursing home, but this time the residents were in their rooms. I could see armor hanging on the walls in their rooms, long retired from their days fighting battles. Then my attention was drawn to the large scroll that sat on each of their dressers. I wondered what they were.

In my vision, the nursing home residents began receiving visitors. When the guests arrived, they got out of their beds with great excitement. The first thing they did was point out the battle attire hanging on the walls. Then, they would go over to the dresser and open up the scroll. With great passion, they would point to the scroll and tell stories.

It now became clear to me who these residents were. I was seeing a picture of older Christian leaders who had fought Great Commission battles during their lifetimes but were now disengaged from the wars. They were satisfied with telling the stories of what happened in the past. I still did not fully understand what the scrolls were, but they seemed to relate to the stories they were telling.

While I was still trying to figure out what was going on with this older generation, the picture changed to the group sitting on couches I had seen the day before. This time, they were at a large banquet table. In front of them was a great feast with wine and a sumptuous spread of food. They were laughing as they indulged in generous helpings of food and wine.

Then my attention turned to a large door at the back of the room. I could tell someone was beating on it from the outside. I was given eyes to see what was outside the door: a great battle being waged. It was a bloody, brutal conflict. There was an invading force, fighting to take over the city. The man knocking on the door of the banquet hall was trying to get the attention of the men and women who were feasting, but they ignored his knocking.

I now understood who this group at the banquet table represented. It was a generation of self-absorbed Christians. Pleasure and entertainment were their primary concerns. I immediately thought of 2 Timothy 3:1–5:

> *But mark this: There will be terrible times in the last days. People will be lovers of themselves, lovers of money, boastful, proud, abusive, disobedient to their parents, ungrateful, unholy, without love, unforgiving, slanderous, without self-control, brutal, not lovers of the good, treacherous, rash, conceited, lovers of pleasure*

rather than lovers of God—having a form of godliness but denying its power.

I cried out, "Lord, how do we wake up this generation?" The answer to my question came to my spirit, "You need to pray."

The scene shifted again to the young army, the millions of young people dressed for battle. This time I could see them on a massive battlefield; there were so many soldiers I couldn't see the end of them. It struck me that many of them were dark-haired and Asian.

They were all dressed for battle but confused about what they should do. I noticed they were all of lower rank, and there were no leaders among them. They were holding the same scrolls I had seen in the nursing home. They would open them up and stare at them. It was clear they couldn't read what they said. They would turn them to the left and to the right and even upside down to understand what was on the scrolls. Then the Lord shifted my attention to the scrolls themselves, and I could see what they were. They were battle plans for the war, laid out with maps of the battlefields.

Now I was beginning to understand what these three scenes meant. The older generation led most of the global missions initiatives. They had learned how to fight and win. But the next generation, those on the couch and the banquet table, didn't continue with the battle plans, because they were too self-absorbed. The young army was signing up to fight, but they weren't clear on how to conduct the battle and lacked leaders to direct them. I realized the battle couldn't be won without the older and younger generations working together. "See, I will send the prophet Elijah to you before that great and dreadful day of the LORD comes. He will turn the hearts of the parents to their children, and the hearts of the children to their parents; or else I will come and strike the land with total destruction" (Malachi 4:5–6).

Day 3: August 14, 2008

The encounter continued into a third day. I woke up with a strong impression to study the book of Joshua. I turned to the first chapter, where the Lord tells an elderly Joshua that is to lead the Israelites as they fight for and inhabit the promised land. This was necessary because of the rebellion of an entire generation of Israelites who refused to know and follow God's ways. Joshua had to lead a young army even though he was 79 years of age.

Another portion of scripture rose up in my heart: Isaiah 59, which tells us about the zeal of the Lord, who is clothed for battle and will destroy His enemies. "From the west, people will fear the name of the LORD, and from the rising of the sun, they will revere his glory. For he will come like a pent-up flood that the breath of the LORD drives along" (Isaiah 59:19).

The Lord was making clear to me that the great conflict at the end of the age was coming. There will be a great harvest in which all the nations of the world will finally be reached (Matthew 24:14) and Israel is saved (Romans 11:26). But Christ will also bring a great judgment against evil on the earth.

While meditating on these scriptures, the scene of the young army reopened in front of me. I again saw tens of millions of young people dressed in armor. Armed with swords and shields, they held their maps but were unable to read the battle plans.

This time I noticed they are all gazing up. I turned my head to see heaven open and the Lord Jesus dressed for battle. He was not seated on His throne, but standing, ready to act.

I looked off into the distance behind the young army, and I could see large hordes of demons gathering and running toward the young army. They were straining themselves to get there quickly. It was clear to me they wanted to destroy this young army before they could understand the battle plans.

Suddenly, I found myself walking in the midst of the young army, explaining the plans to them. I understood that I represented all the older Joshuas who have been called to help lead this massive young army. As I walked among the young soldiers, I could tell they were learning very quickly. It was like they had been waiting for this missing piece.

We were then interrupted by a horn. It sounds again and again, louder and louder, like many shofars all blowing at the same time. The battle was beginning. I found myself walking quickly through the lines of soldiers, saying, "It is time! It is time! It is time!" They seemed to understand what was happening and all stood at attention, ready to move into battle.

This encounter on the third day lasted into the afternoon. When it was finished, I sat in our bedroom chair, writing down the details of what had just happened. I tried to understand what it all meant but realized full understanding might not come until much later.

In the days and weeks that followed, I shared my experience with other Christian leaders, looking for confirmation and advice. Key leaders in the body of Christ, people with depth and maturity whom I trust, confirmed that the encounter was from the Lord and that it had to do with what was about to come. I then shared the details of my encounter with friends who lead prayer movements; I asked them to intercede for all three generations that God's will would be done. Karen and I committed all of this to the Lord and reaffirmed our commitment to Christ's leadership, wherever He might lead us.

It is my hope as you read this book that you will find the inspiration and boldness to move to the next level in your walk with Jesus and your assignment in the Great Commission.

Introduction

We Are in a Battle

The Bible is, by far, the most widely distributed and studied book in the world—and for good reason. The Word of God gives meaning to everything in life. It explains humanity's original purpose, God's design for the family, and universal principles of justice. It defines right and wrong, leads us to salvation, and shows us a glimpse of eternity.

One of the main themes of the Bible is the war between good and evil. It's a battle between the armies of heaven and the powers of hell. This is a real and tangible war that has been waged since creation, and you and I are right in the middle of it. We will not just be caught up in this battle, we will fight it.

There's an ancient proverb that says, "See no evil, hear no evil, speak no evil." Many people live their lives like this, pretending there is no unseen battle or evil kingdom, thinking that if they ignore its reality, they won't be affected. But from Genesis to Revelation, the Bible is full of heavenly and earthly conflicts.

In the beginning, God created the heavens and the earth, and then the earth's inhabitants. On the sixth day, he made man in His image to rule over His creation. Shortly thereafter, God's plan was challenged by Satan, who came in the form of a serpent to tempt Adam and Eve to disobey the Lord. The result is what we call the Fall, and it dramatically affected God's original plan for His good creation.

There is no question that all three parties—Satan, Adam, and Eve—could accept or resist God's will. They were free moral agents in a cosmic battle, and so are we. This presupposition is woven through all of the books of the Old Testament. A spiritual warfare worldview is even more prevalent in the New Testament, where the ministry of Jesus and His followers is defined by tearing down Satan's kingdom and building the kingdom of heaven. Peter summarized Jesus's ministry by saying Jesus "went about doing good and healing all who were oppressed by the devil" (Acts 10:38 NKJV).

Jesus's ministry shows us that God's purposes for the world have to be fought for and won. This is why Jesus had to die on a cross, descend to the lower regions, be resurrected, and sit at the right hand of His Father. These actions defeated the principalities and powers (Colossians 2:14–15).

What Jesus began in His ministry must now be advanced by His church, applying the victory He secured to the ends of the earth. We call this the Great Commission, and it's our primary mandate as believers in the church age.

The ebb and flow of this battle is the primary theme of the Gospels, the book of Acts, and the New Testament Epistles. The world is still largely in bondage to the evil one. We have the authority in Christ and the power of the Holy Spirit to tear down his strongholds and see people set free, but only if we are willing to engage in the war.

When Jesus returns, He will come "with justice [as] he judges and wages war" (Revelation 19:11), and He will be followed by the armies of heaven. When the apostle John saw a vision of the scene, he recorded, "Coming out of his mouth is a sharp sword with which to strike down the nations" (v. 15). The ultimate victory will be won by Jesus, but until that time we need to be trained and active as soldiers, taking ground as we help advance Christ's kingdom. This war is not imaginary; it is quite real.

Avoid engaging in this battle, and it's a sure guarantee you will be a casualty. Evil forces have no pity on those who are passive and defenseless. What we call the church today in much of the world has become a loose-knit fellowship, participating in religious services but largely unengaged with—or unaware of—the spiritual battle taking place all around them. Many churchgoers are just trying to find out how to make it through life. In many cases, they're just looking to survive.

Often the enemy attacks at will, with little or no resistance, leaving people wounded and even destroyed. Christian leadership tries to pick up the pieces and bring some level of healing. But is this really what God intended His church to be?

Are you ready to turn this situation around? Are you tired of powerless religion that provides very few real answers? Do you want to go on the offense and see the enemy defeated in your personal life, your family, and society itself? If so, then this book is for you.

Chapter 1

Becoming a Jesus Freak

It all started when I was twelve years old and began to encounter God. Prior to this experience, I was completely unaware of the supernatural. All I knew about God was what I had heard in church on Sunday mornings.

Every week it was almost exactly the same. The service started at 11:00 a.m. precisely. There was always a hymn or two from the church hymnal, a repeated liturgy, and a fifteen-minute sermon, which concluded with the same benediction each week, promptly at noon. At home I never saw anyone read the large family Bible that rested on a stand and was kept on a table in the corner of our living room. The only public prayer I experienced was when faithful members from church would repeat the Lord's Prayer or when my father would recite a short, memorized dinner prayer in Swedish. It's not that my church community didn't believe the Bible or in the importance of prayer, but they were raised with the idea that such things were meant only for Sunday church and weren't relevant to everyday life.

In 1963, Mom and Dad moved our family from one suburb of Minneapolis, Minnesota, to another, which meant we needed to find a new local church to attend. My parents didn't have any particular spiritual criteria in mind, just a conviction that "we should go to church." Soon, we found a church that was a part of the same denomination as our previous church, and it was close to our new house. That made my mother happy.

My parents always tried to do the right thing. They were honest, hardworking, and had strong moral convictions. When I turned eleven years old, they made sure I was part of the confirmation class at our new church. Confirmation is a tradition in Catholic and many Protestant churches meant to help a young person understand their faith. In my case, these classes were not very exciting, and as far as I could tell, no one in my class had a personal relationship with Jesus. In fact, the young pastor who led the confirmation class introduced all of us to drinking alcohol. Needless to say, there wasn't a strong presence of the Holy Spirit.

I was counting the days until these boring classes would be over and I could leave the church. It wasn't that I didn't care about God, but like most young people, I wasn't excited about dry religion. Finally, just after my twelfth birthday, confirmation day came. This was the day when we would put on our white gowns, sit on stage, and recite our commitment of confirmation as part of the graduation ceremony. I didn't know that God was going to use this occasion to surprise me with His presence.

The sanctuary of our two-hundred-seat church was beautiful, complete with hardwood pews, vaulted ceilings, and numerous stained glass windows. But while the building had plenty of aesthetic appeal, it was neither well-ventilated nor air-conditioned—and the day of my confirmation was unusually warm. Up on that stage, underneath our white gowns, we boys wore dress pants, Oxford shirts, and ties borrowed from our dads. We were all sweating profusely, and we couldn't help but notice that every eye in the room was fixed upon us, watching our every move.

The confirmation ceremony started with a back-and-forth public response. The pastor began, "In testimony of this faith and confession, I now ask you: Do you believe in God, the Father Almighty, in Jesus Christ, His only Son our Lord, and in the Holy Spirit?"

We responded in unison, "Yes, I believe."

The pastor then asked, "Do you believe that Jesus Christ, true God and true man, is your Lord?"

We responded, "Yes, I believe."

"Do you believe that you are a sinner?"

"Yes, I believe."

"Do you believe that Jesus Christ died for you and shed His blood for you on the cross for the forgiveness of all your sins?"

"Yes, I believe."

A strange, warm, presence began to move through my body. I found myself teary-eyed as I was publicly confessing "I believe" on the stage that Sunday morning. I had no explanation, no framework for what was happening to me, but a rush of joy flooded my heart. As I opened my eyes and looked around, I loved everybody in a new way.

My initial thought was that this was normal, that all the kids must have been touched in the same way too, but I soon realized that wasn't the case at all. The other boys in the class had hidden straws and spit balls under their gowns and were shooting them at each other on stage. *Was I the only one who felt the presence of God?*

In the weeks that followed, I was not the same person. Out of nowhere, I had an urge to find a Bible and begin reading it. Every verse came alive, even though I didn't fully understand all the King James language. I started to give away my allowance and lawn mowing money when I saw a need. My friends thought I was crazy and were constantly reminding me how much candy I could have bought if I hadn't given all my money away.

Because I had never seen anyone in my house read the Bible, I would only read it while hiding in my bed at night, sometimes with a flashlight under the covers. I had no Christian friends, and to my knowledge, nobody walked with the Lord in my family yet. There was no one to disciple me at our church. I felt completely alone.

Despite not having someone in my life who could help me to grow in the Lord, I had a strong sense of God's abiding presence. I hadn't though much about sin before, but now when I did something I knew was wrong, I felt guilty. Later on, I would learn that it was the Holy Spirit within me, teaching me and convicting me of sin. My old, sinful habits just weren't fun anymore.

Even after my real encounter with the Lord, I had begun to slowly fall away. Without Christian friends or a community to be part of, I didn't grow in my faith. By high school, I fell back into the typical public school scene.

Many of my relationships in junior high and then high school were defined by how much we could drink or what girl we could go out with. My sports teams would gather over the weekends at parties where we would get drunk, and any relationships with girls were about seeing how far we could go on a date. In the classroom, we would cheat our way through the hard classes. Everybody thought we were cool, and as the popular athletes in the school, we felt on top of the world.

Jesus Freak

I still found the parties and went on plenty of dates, but instead of getting drunk and pushing boundaries, I was talking about Jesus. This made my friends and dates extremely uncomfortable. Some of my football friends immediately abandoned me. My popularity dropped like a rock, and some people completely disappeared from my life. They thought I had lost my mind.

One of my closest high school friends said it this way, "Mark, what's wrong with you? You're six foot three, first-string on the football and wrestling teams, the girls are after you, and now you're talking about religion? You even carry around your Bible at school. What are you—some kind of Jesus Freak?" From that point on, this friend disappeared too.

There were a few who respected what was happening in my life. They would ask me probing questions about God's existence and why there is evil in the world. This frustrated me, because I didn't have answers. No one had yet taught or discipled me in any way, and my knowledge of the Bible was still quite limited. I had a lot of zeal but very little knowledge.

It wasn't until the eleventh grade that I met someone else who was walking with Jesus. I had started attending Jesus rallies, gatherings of young people with contemporary worship and speakers who had come out of the hippie movement of the

1960s. This was all a part of what mainstream media labeled "The Jesus People movement," then sweeping across America. These "Jesus People" or "Jesus Freaks," as some people called them, had testimonies about finding Jesus, being filled with the Holy Spirit, and being delivered from drugs and immoral lifestyles. It was at one of these meetings that I met an old football buddy, Kirk. Hungry for God and desiring to know the truth, we decided to start hanging out together to read the Bible. Burning our incense and candles into the night, we would read books like Psalms and Proverbs, discussing them like philosophers for hours.

"Man, have you read this one?" Kirk would say, pointing to a proverb.

"Wow, that is cool!" I would respond.

It seemed like the Bible was a treasure chest we could open every night in our search for truth. The Word brought life to my soul, gave me a reason to live, and ignited hope for my future. "Blessed are those who hunger and thirst for righteousness, for they will be filled" (Matthew 5:6).

I had a Bible called *The Way*, which was written in big block letters on its paperback cover. In addition to the sixty-six books of the Bible, it contained testimonies from young people. *The Way* was easy to read and understand, and was relevant to my everyday life. I underlined all my favorite verses, and I could sense God was speaking to me through His Word. Don't copy the behavior and customs of this world, but be a new and different person with a fresh newness in all you do and think. Then you will learn from your own experience how his ways will really satisfy you." (Romans 12:2).

Mom and Dad, I Found Jesus for Real, and He's Changed My Life

By this time, I had formally left my parent's church and was attending Bible studies and prayer meetings three or four nights a week. I was sharing my newfound faith with everyone. My dad and mom couldn't understand why our local family church wasn't good enough for their son and were deeply disappointed I wasn't going to church with them anymore. Being the only child still at home, I had my parents' undivided attention. They had become concerned about the drastic lifestyle changes I was making. Instead of late night parties, I was now going to worship gatherings and home Bible studies. What normal teenager was doing that?

My identity had been entirely wrapped up in sports and being one of the star athletes on the varsity football and wrestling teams. Now, I didn't really care about sports, and that just didn't make any sense to my parents. Since I was a young boy I had dreamed of playing college football, and much of my spare time growing up was spent playing sports and bodybuilding with my best friend, Jamie. Now my mom and dad were concerned I had joined a cult and had somehow been brainwashed. What had happened to their son?

About this time, my family was in complete upheaval. Taking after my grandfather, my dad was now a full-on alcoholic and had already received two DWIs. My mom was worried and completely stressed out over what was happening with Dad. But she was also worried about my older sister, Judy, who was in the middle of a divorce from her husband.

At age fifteen, Judy found herself pregnant and ended up marrying her boyfriend. They lived next door to us, and in twelve years, they had nine children. Their family problems and household chaos were always close at hand, and it seemed a new drama was unfolding every day, spilling over into our lives. Some days, it seemed our family was living in its very own soap opera.

In her pain, Judy turned to new age mysticism to find comfort. She began attending meditation parties where she and her friends would take turns levitating and reading the teachings of Edgar Cayce, a new age philosopher and psychic. When I would try to talk to Judy and her oldest daughter Christine about Jesus, they would just laugh out loud, making fun of me.

My initial response towards my dysfunctional family was to stay away, but God convicted me that I needed to pray for them and find a way to introduce them to Jesus. Being the youngest in the family, I felt dismissed and put down. My brothers and sister were older and knew more, so why should they listen to their baby brother who was acting so weird? But I was convinced that only in Jesus could they find true peace and happiness. I was determined not to give up.

One day my mom and dad sat me down at the kitchen table and, with a very serious tone, asked, "What is this religious movement that you are a part of? Why did you leave our church? Are you in a cult?" They were sincerely worried about their youngest son. My lifestyle changes had been abrupt and dramatic. They had been used to the drinking and the parties, and they accepted these as normal, but this new spiritual behavior was beyond their understanding.

They sat patiently, waiting for my answer. I paused carefully to measure my response to their questions and replied, "Mom, Dad, I found Jesus for real, and He's changed my life."

"What do you mean?" they asked. "You were raised in church and went through confirmation. We believe in Jesus. We're Christians. We live a good life and help people. Every Sunday we go to church, and we've done so our whole lives."

My parents were some of the humblest and most loving people I've ever known. Both of them would give the shirt off their back to someone in need. We had a large family, and every week it seemed someone would come to our house asking for food, clothes, or to "borrow" money. My mom and dad never turned anyone away.

I remember once when two young men—complete strangers—knocked on our door on a Saturday morning while we were eating breakfast. They said they were selling something, though I can't recall what. My mother didn't think twice and quickly asked these "nice young men" to come in and join us. She made her traditional scrambled eggs, bacon, toast with strawberry jam, and coffee. Our two guests ate everything in sight. You see, my parents treated everyone with great love and respect, no matter how rich or poor, no matter their skin color or religion. This day was no different. My parents treated these strangers like their own kids, feeding them and making small talk. And then, after breakfast, they sent them on their way. A few minutes later, my dad happened to be looking out the window and watched his own car backing out of our gravel driveway. Those two "nice young men" were stealing the family car. Even when my father had to call the police to report the theft, both of my parents refused to press charges.

"I am not talking about church; I am talking about a relationship with God Himself. I have become born again." I replied. Then I turned my attention to my parents, "Dad, Mom, look at what is happening to our family. It's falling apart. Dad, you get drunk daily. Mom, you cry yourself to sleep every night. Our whole family needs to encounter Jesus in a new way."

Now my parents were listening intently. They were getting desperate, and I knew they saw the changes in my life. They noticed that I had become more respectful of them and had quit getting drunk at parties. In the days that followed, I continued to talk to them about what it meant to have a personal relationship with Jesus.

First, Mom came to me. It was late one night while Dad was at work; he always worked the graveyard shift at the Minneapolis *Star and Tribune*. She said, "As far back as I can remember, I have believed in God. I say my prayers daily, but I don't have what you have. Would you help me?" We both had tears in our eyes as I led her through a prayer of surrender to Christ. Mom then looked up and cried out loud, "Ohhhh, Jesus! I love you!" She started laughing and gave me a long hug.

From that point on, Mom lived with a daily peace and truly demonstrated the fruit of the Spirit in every area of her life. Later, when I pastored, she served as the head of the Sunday school and loved the children like her own. They would all call her Grandma Anderson, because of the unconditional love she demonstrated so well and freely gave away. She had many "adopted" children and grandchildren. Both of my parents had a large capacity for love.

A few weeks later, I led my father to Christ. He too had a dramatic encounter. The next week, he started Christian counseling to find freedom from his alcohol addiction. It was just a month later when he came home from one of his appointments and announced to me with a smile on his face, "I am filled with the Holy Spirit!" He was free from alcohol and had a whole new demeanor.

Both my parents asked for Bibles and started reading them daily. My dad signed up for just about every Christian ministry mailing list he could find. At one point, I counted fifty-two ministries he was supporting. Though he didn't have much money, it seemed like he couldn't give away enough to help other people. In the 1980s my mom and dad became anchors in one of my church plants in inner-city Minneapolis.

After my mom and dad were born again, my sister, Judy, followed. She was always spiritually sensitive, but now she was a radical for Jesus. One night, we built a bonfire behind her house and burned all of her new age books and materials. Her oldest daughter, Christine, also came to the Lord and immediately turned into an evangelist, talking to everybody in the family about Jesus. Judy's oldest son, Scott, worked for me in ministry and became a missionary to India. Later he became a key leader in the body of Christ, working around the world. One by one, my family members were coming to Christ.

My Future Wife

During my junior year in high school, I was friends with a beautiful young woman named Karen. We had known each other since the second grade and had grown up attending the same schools and living in the same neighborhoods. I would regularly talk to her about Jesus at the bus stop and at school, but she thought I was crazy. It was hard for me to witness to her, because she knew way more Scripture than I did. She had grown up in a church where they studied the Bible and was even on a Bible quiz team. For some reason, she and some of her friends had walked away from all of that and had given themselves over to the high school party scene.

I used to regularly invite Karen to come with me to Jesus rallies. She said no again and again, but to my surprise, in the spring of 1975 she finally said yes. On that Friday night, she was deeply moved by the sermon, but she didn't respond to the altar call. She later told me that she tossed and turned all night. She described that night as a "battle for her soul." Early the next morning in her bedroom, after a restless night, she gave her life to Jesus.

The following Sunday, she came with me to another meeting. This time, we both went forward in response to an invitation to be filled with the Holy Spirit. Neither of us knew what being filled with the Holy Spirit meant or what to expect, but our spiritual hunger was soaring.

One of the leaders laid hands on us, and we immediately began to pray in an unknown language. We were laughing and were filled with a joy neither of us had ever experienced. When we left the service, we laughed all the way home to my parents' house, where we had lunch. After lunch, we went into the backyard and started laughing again. We couldn't—and didn't want to—stop. This lasted for hours. "For the kingdom of God is not a matter of eating and drinking, but of righteousness, peace and joy in the Holy Spirit" (Romans 14:17).

In the days that followed, we felt like different people. We had new power to live for God, prayer was easier, and we wanted to worship any time we had the chance. We were filled with a zeal for missions and wanted to reach everyone, everywhere.

Soon Karen and I became more than friends. We began to consider that perhaps God was leading us to spend our lives together. We spent hours with each other worshiping, praying, and developing strategies to reach people we knew who were lost.

"Let's make a list!" I declared one afternoon during our prayer time.

"A list of what?" Karen asked.

"A list of all our family members who don't know the Lord. We can pray for them and witness to them until they're all Christians," I stated. We began to make a list, and soon we had thirty-two names. In the months that followed, all thirty-two of these people came to Christ!

Our Life and Possessions Not Our Own

In June of 1976, Karen and I were married, and we moved into our first apartment in Minneapolis. It was a modest, one-bedroom apartment with green shag carpet, and we soon discovered the place was infested with cockroaches. But many of the people in the apartment complex were Christians involved in the growing Jesus People movement in our city. We found a thriving spiritual community and it was an exciting place to live.

After setting up our apartment, our newly saved nephews and nieces started bringing their friends over to hear about Jesus. Many of them came to Christ. We found ourselves discipling people our age or younger seven days a week. We always seemed to have at least one person living with us who had just come to Christ and was getting their life in order.

It was sometimes challenging and perhaps not the best way to start our newly married life, but our lives did not belong to us. There was usually someone sleeping on our living room couch or on a floor somewhere or even in our bathtub. Some were getting out of a sexually immoral lifestyle; others were leaving behind drugs or alcohol. We were living church 24/7, and our little apartment was the gathering place. They would eat our food, use up our shampoo, and invite their drug-addicted friends to our meetings. We were riding on a move of God that today is remembered as the Jesus People movement.

It was exciting and there seemed to be something new happening every day. God was at work, and young people in our city and across America were hungry for Him. There was never a dull moment.

Consumed with Leading People to Christ

For Karen and me, it was normal to lead people to Jesus. Our family members, people at work, friends at school, and even strangers on the street were coming to Christ. I was so consumed with evangelism, I would sometimes drive back and forth between Minneapolis and St. Cloud, Minnesota, on Friday and Sunday nights, picking up hitchhikers who attended the St. Cloud State University. Another time, I prayed, "Lord I need a better car. You see that I'm driving all the time, picking people up for meetings and church services. I need something newer and with better gas mileage." I was eighteen years old and had little money, but God led me to a three-year-old, beautiful red Pontiac Le Mans, which I was able to buy for $400. Once I had them in the car, they had to stay there for an hour. My glove box was conveniently filled with Bible tracts. Many times, I would be able to lead them in a prayer for salvation at the end of our drive.

Karen and I were both working daytime jobs, unlike some of our newly saved friends and relatives. Some of them were out of work, so they stayed at our apartment all day while we were gone. We would experience minor but annoying inconveniences with our "houseguests." One morning, we got up to make ourselves breakfast before work while most of our guests were still sleeping. The day before, we had purchased a dozen eggs, but Karen couldn't find them. Looking at me, she said, "What is happening to all of our eggs?" I replied, "I don't know. We just bought them yesterday." Later we found out that one of our newly saved nephews used eggs along with our shampoo to give his hair more body.

Karen worked full-time at General Mills and would return home in the evening to a growing pile of dirty dishes overflowing in the sink. These kinds of inconveniences occurred nearly every day. Sometimes we felt like we were parents to a house full of homeless young people, but we were only twenty years old ourselves, still figuring out our own lives.

We were in a season when God was teaching us to surrender everything to Him, even the small things. That meant sacrificing our time, our comfort, our money, our food, our shampoo, and even our eggs. Nothing was just "ours" anymore, and everything was shared or given freely. It wasn't easy, and we didn't do everything right, but the Lord was teaching us what a surrendered life ought to look like—and a surrendered life always means making some kind of sacrifice. As newly married young Christians, Karen and I would read the great faith stories of men and women who did amazing things for God, people like Hudson Taylor, Amy Carmichael, T. L. Osborn, and Billy Graham. These heroes did great things, often with tremendous cost, and we aspired to be like them.

In those days, it seemed everyone was talking about Jesus. In the early days of the Jesus People movement, *Time* magazine put a stylized drawing of Jesus on the cover, along with the caption,

"The Jesus Revolution." The Holy Spirit was sweeping across America, and even the secular media had to acknowledge the spiritual awakening taking place. We were watching modern day miracles as people were freed from destructive, sinful lifestyles, drug addictions, and demonic strongholds. We had personally experienced and witnessed the outpouring of the Spirit in our own lives and were helping spread that fire everywhere we went. "For Karen and me, there was no going back. Our lives were changed forever."

What we were learning as a young married couple was the training we would need for the larger battles God was preparing us to fight. It was raw, and we didn't always do things perfectly, but we were learning how to be faithful in the small things. "You have been faithful with a few things; I will put you in charge of many things" (Matthew 25:21).

We were typical Christian young people who wanted to be part of the great adventure of missions, even though we had no idea what real missionary work was. We had studied spiritual warfare, read lots of books, and could even quote some of the main principles presented by heroes of faith, but we had not really fought any major battles. We were about to graduate from boot camp to the battlefield.

Chapter 2:

God, What am I Doing?

It was a frigid early March day in Grand Forks, North Dakota. Thirty-mile-per-hour crosswinds blew a thin blanket of snow across the highway. My wife Karen and I had been listening to the weather forecast on our car radio on our drive up from Minneapolis, and we knew a blizzard was coming. Such weather was not unusual in this part of America. Still, we talked about how the storm might affect our plans. You don't want to get stuck driving on the highway during a blizzard, especially in North Dakota. It could be dangerous.

Karen and I were just twenty years old at the time. We had been invited to visit an evangelist named Lowell Lundstrom, who was currently on tour in North Dakota, one of the coldest places in the US. Our friend Joe, Lowell's ministry pilot, was given the assignment of recruiting a campaign coordinator. Joe thought of me, and that's how, a few weeks later, we found ourselves traveling straight north into the unknown. The loose job description for a campaign coordinator, as we found out later, was someone who would travel to a city before Lowell Lundstrom and his team arrived to prepare the community and organize the details of the ministry campaign. This included bringing local churches together in support of the event, raising the necessary funds, securing an appropriate venue and sound system, plus doing anything else required for the event to happen.

We drove behind the auditorium and pulled up next to a large Greyhound bus with "The Lundstroms" painted along both sides. There was no doubt we were in the right place. The bus looked like it should belong to a country and western band rather than a singing evangelist. It had darkened windows with a small American flag on the back. On the side, under their name, was a picture of a guitar. Country music and culture were not our thing, and suddenly I felt out of place. All at once, I felt like I was in a different world.

We trudged through the snow up to the bus door and began to knock. No one answered, so we pounded harder and harder. Finally, the bus door squealed open and the evangelist's little brother Leroy, a smiling redheaded man, greeted us. "Hi," I said. "I'm Mark Anderson, and this is my wife, Karen. We're here to see Lowell."

We were ushered up the steps to the small circular sitting area at the front of the bus. Remnants of an afternoon snack were still on the table—crackers, cheeses and something that looked like the remains of a "hot dish," a popular meal that included a variety of ingredients mixed together and baked, sometimes with cheese, and topped with dried onion rings or crushed cereal. It was one way my own mother would use leftovers so food wasn't wasted.

Meeting Lowell

A moment later, Lowell came out from the back of the bus, tightening his belt as he walked. He was six foot one, about two hundred pounds, and had deep, penetrating blue eyes. His hair was a little flat on one side, like he had just woken up from a nap. "Hi, I'm Lowell Lundstrom." He grabbed my hand and gave it a tight squeeze, "You're the two from Minneapolis that Joe talked about, right?"

I answered, "Yes, we just drove up from the Twin Cities."

"Great," Lowell said. "I have to get ready for tonight's show, so why don't you sit near the front of the auditorium and afterward we will go out for dinner together?" I later found out that dinner was always after the evening show, often around eleven o'clock in the evening.

Over the next few hours, we watched as the three-thousand-seat Civic Center in Grand Forks filled up with families and young people all coming to see Lowell and his band. A big fan of Elvis Presley, Lowell had started a country rock 'n' roll band at age fourteen, and at fifteen was radically converted to Christ. After attending Bible college, he went back to his natural gifting of music, songwriting, and preaching, and started Lowell Lundstrom Ministries. His ministry drew people with country gospel music, but he would always include a gospel message and an altar call.

At about nine o'clock that evening, Lowell gave the altar call. Teary-eyed, I watched hundreds of children, teenagers, and families come forward and surrender to Jesus. Large groups of high school students walked forward together, the teenage girls arm in arm. After reaching the front, some of them knelt down on the gymnasium floor. We even noticed what looked like whole families coming forward. Karen and I were amazed to see so many responding. I was hooked. I wanted to be a part of this for the rest of my life, to reach as many people as possible with the message of Jesus. I knew this is what I was made for.

We waited patiently after the altar call to reconnect with Lowell and his team. Karen and I met Lowell and the band at a local truck stop at about 10:30 p.m. that night. Karen, who usually goes to bed early and gets up at six the next morning for work was already tired. Newly pregnant, she was fighting to keep her eyes open as she sat at the table, waiting for her dinner.

After ordering chicken-fried steak, a basket of ribs, and a wide assortment of truck stop food, we started to talk. Lowell had on his blue polyester blazer with western-style collar and cowboy boots. He looked straight at me with his piercing blue eyes and said, "So, you want to be a campaign coordinator?"

I wasn't completely sure what a campaign coordinator was just yet, so I paused for a moment, trying to figure out an intelligent answer. "That would be great. I love evangelism," I replied.

Lowell smiled, "Good. You'll start tomorrow. The ministry plane is flying to Bismarck in the afternoon. You can go with the other coordinators." I glanced over at my wife, who had an alarmed look on her face, wondering what had just happened. We thought we were coming just to check things out and ask questions, not to start a new job immediately.

New Job

Not wanting to lose the opportunity to become part of the ministry staff, I turned to Lowell and told him it sounded great. Lowell stuck out his hand to shake mine. "Welcome to Lundstrom Ministries!" he said. Just like that—without any discussion of how much money I would make, where we would live, or what a coordinator did exactly—I had a new job.

After dinner, Karen and I left the restaurant, ventured back into the cold wind, and got into our 1971 Plymouth Duster. Even before I could start the car, Karen began asking questions. "What just happened? Where are we going to live? What about me? I can't go to Bismarck. I have to get home and go to work in the morning. It's a seven-hour drive. What about your job? Are you just going to quit? That doesn't seem responsible. You didn't even ask him how much you're going to be paid? The weather forecast says a blizzard is on the way, and you want me to drive back, alone and pregnant?" All of Karen's questions were valid, and I couldn't answer a single one.

I turned to my pregnant wife and tried to reassure her that everything was going to be fine and that all of her questions would be answered. But my words did nothing to relieve the tension. Karen felt I wasn't being responsible, and she didn't agree with what looked like a rash decision on my part. We were still newly married and hadn't yet learned how to wait on the Lord or listen for Him to speak to us on important decisions.

The next morning, we checked out of our hotel. I would fly to Bismarck in the Lundstrom Ministry's Cessna 172 and Karen would begin her seven-hour drive home, alone, through a blizzard. Quietly she left, but first she gave me a look I had never seen before. I had forced my strong will to get what I wanted, and she knew there was nothing she could do to change my mind. She had never been a complainer, but with that look she was letting me know she wasn't happy at all this was happening.

I'm sure if I had been more mature, I would have handled all of this much differently. But I was consumed with excitement about the potential adventure that lay ahead and just figured everything would work out. Out of God's mercy and grace, it eventually did.

But later on I realized how immature and selfish I had been in the process—and how patient the Lord can be.

How Am I Going to Explain This to My Wife?

Despite my mistakes, somehow I knew deep within my heart that the journey we were about to begin was ordained by God. More than that, I had a strange sense we were connected to something bigger than either of us—some kind of master plan that was multi-generational. But in the moment, I felt like someone who had just jumped in the deep end with nothing to hold on to. I was walking into this storyline blind, without understanding and without many answers.

That evening, I arrived in Bismarck, North Dakota. To my chagrin, it was even colder than Grand Forks. I'm from Minneapolis, so I'm used to cold temperatures, but this was another level of cold entirely. I couldn't help but think about the early settlers who first came to this region of the country. They must have come in summertime, because they surely wouldn't have stayed if they had known the winters were like this.

Three other staff members and I were picked up at the small, private airport and driven to a roadside Holiday Inn in serious need of redecorating. As we were checking in at the counter, I asked the other members of the team, "So, what happens tomorrow?" They explained they had various committee meetings and training seminars. They had no idea what to do with me. Apparently, Lowell had not given them any instructions. They weren't even sure who I was.

Over the next six weeks I bounced around from city to city in North Dakota, trying to just show up and be useful. I talk with Karen every day. I still had no answers for her questions. I had not received any training, and no one had explained what I was supposed to be doing as a campaign coordinator. I had no idea where we were going to live, and there had been no mention of a salary.

Sisseton, South Dakota

Three weeks later, I caught up with Lowell at his headquarters in the tiny town of Sisseton, South Dakota. I drove down from Bismarck with another coordinator named Chet. Being friendly and talkative, Chet gave me coordinator pointers on our five-hour drive. Informal though it was, it was the first "training" of any kind I'd received. He assured me that everything would be okay and that all my questions would eventually be answered. I asked Chet about the town of Sisseton, but he seemed to dodge my questions. He had a way of putting a positive spin on everything.

On the outskirts of Sisseton, I walked into the warehouse-style office of Lundstrom Ministries. I quickly found the small waiting area and stayed put until Lowell arrived. He didn't really have his own office, because he lived on the road most of the year. His mother, Madge, was the ministry administrator, and she was faithful to oversee operations behind the scenes. I can still picture her in the conference room she used as her office with dozens of piles of paper spread across a large table.

Lowell walked into the waiting area and greeted me "How has it been going?" he asked. Lowell was a very optimistic man with a fun-loving and friendly personality. I didn't want to sound negative, and I struggled to answer. Should I be honest? The truth was that the past six weeks had been extremely confusing. I had no idea what I was doing.

"Lowell, can I ask you a few questions?" I began.

He cheerily replied, "Sure!"

I slouched forward on the yellow-colored vinyl couch, nervously asking the big questions. "As staff, where am I supposed to live?" I asked.

"Right here," he replied. "We'll let you move into one of our trailer houses." Driving up to the office, I had seen the trailer houses. They were at least twenty years old, in disrepair, and parked on the edge of a farmer's cornfield. I had also heard that Sisseton was the poorest city in South Dakota, situated in the northeast corner of the state on a Native American reservation, which had its own unique character and challenges.

My mind started racing. How was I going to make this attractive to Karen? She was willing to live lean and was generally a content woman. But a dilapidated trailer next to a cornfield in the corner of South Dakota wasn't anyone's dream home. And the winters would be even colder than they were in Minneapolis.

I asked my next question, "So what do I get paid to be a coordinator?"

Lowell replied, "We can give you $6,000 a year and, of course, we'll let you drive one of our cars." Together, Karen and I had been making two and a half times that amount in Minneapolis. Once again, I was asking myself the question: *How am I going to explain this to my wife?* Karen worked at General Mills, a major corporation well known for taking care of their employees and offering great benefits.

A few minutes later, Lowell and I walked out the side door of the warehouse/office to what looked like a cross between a junkyard and a used car lot. We walked over to the gravel parking lot to a 1965 Oldsmobile. It was covered in snow but rust showed through on the tire wells. Lowell gave me the keys with a smile, explaining that one of the staff would show me my trailer house later. The driver's door creaked as I opened it. I put the key in the ignition, turned it partway, and looked at the odometer. It read 211,000 miles.

Lowell then said goodbye, and I sat in the car thinking, *What am I doing?* At that instant, a large wind gust came and snow from the roof fell off and hit my face. Any thought of glamour or of some grand adventure dissipated. I prayed, "Lord, we are selling out for You. I know You are real. I trust You will use our lives for Your glory."

Our Leap of Faith

I went back into the warehouse, found a phone, and called Karen, trying my best to put a positive spin on what I'd just learned. A few days later, I drove back to Minneapolis. After praying together, we felt the Lord was telling us we needed to take this leap of faith. Even though many of our questions were still unanswered and nothing was glamorous about the move, we said yes.

Later that week, Karen resigned from her well-paying job at General Mills, and we gave notice on our apartment. We packed up everything and moved to a trailer house on a Native American reservation in Sisseton, South Dakota. We felt we were in the middle of God's will, but we really didn't have a clue as to what our future was going to look like.

The Trailer House

We quickly found out what winters were like in our trailer. There were gaps in the windows everywhere, and it seemed as though half the year there were forty-mile-per-hour winds with drifting snow. In January, it was so cold that if we left anything out on the kitchen counter overnight it would freeze. One night we forgot to put away a gallon of milk and it had ice floating in it the morning.

We learned to have a sense of humor about our run-down lodging—even the mice. It wasn't uncommon to hear the mouse traps going off during the night. One time, we turned on the oven to bake dinner and, minutes later, the trailer filled with smoke and the worst smell you can imagine—something like roast mouse. Another time, while we were sleeping, a mouse ran across Karen and down the bed. She woke up screaming, but when we both realized what had just happened, we started laughing.

Across America

Little did we know that these would be some of the most fulfilling years of our lives. We were on the road countless hours. We learned to love the Minnesota forests, the mountains and plains of the Dakotas and Montana, the Colorado Rockies, and the rainy, deep-green woods of the Pacific Northwest. Every city was a new challenge filled with adventure. Karen was able to meet new friends, and I was satisfying my need to continually conquer something new.

We were hungry for God and His Word. So, with all that time in the car, we listened to the Bible on cassette, teaching messages, and worship music. It was like having our own mobile Bible school, and we grew spiritually as we traveled from city to city.

We were beginning to learn something necessary and very important. It wasn't money, prestige, or comfort that brought happiness; it was being in the middle of God's will. All across America, we were seeing young people and whole families come to Christ. There is no better feeling than, night after night, seeing the stage surrounded by people repenting and turning to Christ. This is what brought us great joy, even if we lived in a dumpy trailer house and drove an old and rusty used car across the highways of America. We loved what we were doing. "But seek first his kingdom and his righteousness, and all these things will be given to you as well" (Matthew 6:33).

The Power of Strategic Prayer

The most powerful prayer of agreement is the prayer of a husband and wife. We had started early in our relationship praying together over our list of family members and friends, and seeing our prayers answered. Now Karen and I were united and on a mission to reach America. There was already a sense that we were part of a young army. We were willing to sacrifice and say yes, even when things didn't make sense. The Bible says, "No one serving as a soldier gets entangled in civilian affairs, but rather tries to please his commanding officer" (2 Timothy 2:4).

"God reveal yourself in this city," I would pray.

"Lord, that's right. Open up their eyes to see," Karen would continue.

We were starting to see how prayer and missions had to go hand in hand. Later on, the Lord would give us an encounter on the other side of the world that would change us the rest of our lives as we learned prayer and missions were meant to be one movement.

Thankfully, after some time I did learn how to direct public campaigns and outreaches. I immersed myself in materials from other ministries, like the Billy Graham Evangelistic Association

(BGEA). I had gone forward during an altar call at a Billy Graham meeting when I was fifteen years old, so I had a special affinity for the famous evangelist. I traveled to their headquarters in my home city of Minneapolis to meet with their directors. They generously gave me copies of all their training materials and later came to speak at some of our schools. They raised the standard for spiritual, moral and financial integrity in ministry. Many of the spiritual principles and values I learned from BGEA back then still impact what I do to this day.

I was getting a crash course in evangelistic outreach ministry. Everything I learned, I immediately put into practice. I studied advertising and marketing, and filled my library with the most up-to-date books and teaching tapes. I received many opportunities to speak at pastoral meetings, committee training events, and church services, and I learned mostly through trial and error. I even learned how to raise money, an important skill set when you have dozens of budgets to meet.

One thing I didn't lack was confidence, and it wasn't long before I had some ideas for reorganizing the Lowell Lundstrom Ministry campaigns. To my great delight, Lowell liked my ideas and allowed me to implement some of them. Not everyone at the Sisseton office was so excited, however. Some of the veteran staff couldn't believe that Lowell had given someone my age the latitude to rewrite campaign processes. Looking back on those days, my confidence could have easily been perceived for arrogance or pride by more mature leaders. Later on, the Lord would have to "pull the slack" out of me and, sometimes, I would learn humility the hard way.

I had convinced Lowell that instead of directing twenty-five small crusades a year, driving by car, I could do a hundred a year if I got my pilot's license. Lowell loved the idea, so I immediately began taking flying lessons locally and logging the required hours to get my pilot's license. I loved being up in the sky and passed my final test the first time. Soon, I was flying with Karen at my right side in the ministry's Cessna 172 single prop plane. In the backseat was our newborn daughter Christelle. Right next to her were our suitcases and my dumbbell weights.

Just as I had promised, we were able to direct four times as many cities by air. Thousands of people were coming to Christ in the campaigns. I was using new methods of advertising and media publicity I had developed through my extensive reading and research. Some days we would fly to one city by breakfast time, usually landing on a private runway, dirt road, or a farmer's field. Then we would fly to a different city by lunch, and on to a third city for the evening, where we would stay overnight.

From 1977 to 1980, we directed more than two hundred citywide evangelistic crusades. Most of the cities were small, rural towns, often with a population of five to ten thousand. They each had a main street, with a single grocery store, a barbershop, a café, a bank, and of course a town square. They usually had one auditorium that could be used for events like ours.

Multi-Generational

During this season, Lowell exposed me to many aspects of ministry, including television production, communications, advertising, etc. Some nights, when we were together in a crusade town, we would stay up late until three or four o'clock in the morning brainstorming how to reach more people for Christ. We were like two excited kids peering eagerly into the candy bag on Halloween night. Lowell had a vision for reaching America, and together we came up with some great ideas. Because he was older than I was, he shared what he knew and let me build on it.

I will always appreciate Lowell and his family, and what I learned as a young man.

This was the late '70s, and during this time I couldn't shake the sense that bigger things lay ahead. I began to get pictures in my spirit during times of prayer: I saw millions of young people across the globe beginning to follow Jesus. Every time I looked at a map or saw a television program about a foreign country, I wanted to go there. Those opportunities were coming sooner than I expected.

Chapter 3

The Test of Faith

integrity: \ in-ˈte-grə-tē \ *noun*, adherence to moral and ethical principles, soundness of moral character, honesty.[1]

Everyone gets tested, and one of my first tests came while I was organizing a campaign in southern Minnesota. This test came when I least expected it. If I had failed this test of the integrity of my heart, I could have been derailed from my calling and wound up on a completely different path.

The Offer

It happened as I was overseeing a campaign city in Minnesota in 1978. Proud to be the youngest coordinator for Lowell Lundstrom Ministries, I was working hard on a successful campaign. People were impressed with my hard work and organizational ability, and I was developing close relationships in the city. One of those relationships was with a businessman on our finance committee named Tom.

Tom owned a successful sporting goods store, and he had a large six-bedroom home, complete with a recreation room that covered the whole lower level. He was a generous man, and I would often stay in one of his extra bedrooms when I came into town to work on the campaign. One morning when I stopped by to pick up some of my belongings, Tom stopped me in the kitchen and asked if I had time to talk with him and his wife.

Tom was a distinguished looking businessman in his mid-forties. His wife, Sue, still had the look of a high school homecoming queen and was a frequent customer at a favorite spa in town. During my visits to their home, the three of us would often stay up late into the evening talking about the Scriptures. They had a hunger for God, and I could tell they were deeply touched and challenged by the lifestyle that our young family was living.

Tom said, "Mark, Sue and I have been talking." I could see Sue nodding her head behind Tom. "We would like to make you an offer. We've been watching you these past months and are very impressed with how you are administering this citywide campaign. We'd like to offer you part ownership in our business and eventually have you take it over." I froze, completely blindsided. I didn't know what to say.

My mind started spinning as different thoughts raced through my head. *Something like this was never in our plans, but what if….? Maybe this is God supplying our needs?* I looked around the gorgeous home, thinking how much I liked nice things. There was a still, small voice in my heart saying, "This is not what I have for you," but the thrill of the offer took over the moment.

"Tom, that is a very generous offer. I love your business. Let me talk to my wife. We will pray about it and get back to you. Would that be okay?"

He replied, "Sure! Take your time. Let me know by the end of the week." Sue walked over and gave me a hug, almost like she was welcoming me into the family.

I raced back out the door, eager to tell Karen. She was waiting patiently outside in our Volkswagen Rabbit (our recent upgrade from the rusty Oldsmobile), staying warm on this cold winter day. Our baby daughter was sleeping soundly in her car seat.

I jumped in the driver's seat and excitedly announced, "Karen, you will never guess what just happened!" Already, I had been quickly overtaken by my young, male pride, thinking about how talented I must be for this successful businessman to make me such an offer. "Tom and Sue want to make me part-owner in their sporting goods business! They want to start more stores all across the country. Eventually, I would be responsible to run the whole business!"

Repentance

Karen looked straight at me without any hesitation and said, "Mark, you know this isn't God. We have been called to be missionaries to the nations. This is a test to see if you can be bought off." In an instant I was completely deflated. Her words cut deep, and I knew she was right. I had almost compromised my calling. Without her there, I probably would have failed the test right then and there, and would have made the biggest mistake of my life.

"After a long pause I swallowed (my pride) and said, "Yeah, you're right." I knew immediately what I had to do. After praying a short prayer with Karen, I stepped out of the car and went back to the house and knocked on the door. Tom and Sue were still in the kitchen finishing their breakfast.

"Do you have a moment?" I asked.

"Sure, come on in," Tom replied.

Over the next ten minutes, I feebly tried to explain why I couldn't accept their offer, describing our global calling the best I could. They were both gracious, but I could tell they thought I was blowing it. How quickly, in their eyes, I had changed from a brilliant, young entrepreneur to a foolish kid.

I humbly walked back to the car, where Karen was waiting, and said, "Karen, we need to pray." Sitting together in our VW, in the circular driveway of this beautiful home, we recommitted our lives to go anywhere and do anything that Jesus asked. The wonderful, tangible presence of God started to fill the car. We turned on some worship music and just began to sing. God knew exactly what He was doing when he gave me Karen. I was amazed at how grounded she already was and how content she could be in any situation. It wouldn't be the first time that the Lord would use my young wife to keep me from making some wrong and costly decision.

I almost lost my calling with the lure of comfort, success, and money. God calls many people into business, and He blesses some financially for his kingdom purposes. But that wasn't my calling. I knew from a young age that I was called to the nations and to reach many people with the gospel of Jesus Christ. At this point I wasn't quite sure what that was going to look like, but I realized I would need to watch the motivations of my heart continually to stay on track.

There Is a Change

We were still enjoying crisscrossing the United States with the Lowell Lundstrom team but were beginning to sense that our time was coming to an end. We had learned so much in three years, but there was this undeniable tug on our hearts for the nations of the world. It wasn't long after we began thinking about a change that we ran into one of the pastors from our Jesus People days.

Roger was a co-founding pastor of a mega-church in the Twin Cities. He also happened to be the preacher who spoke at the service the night Karen gave her life to the Lord. Roger had been an drug dealer before having a radical encounter with the Lord. He became one of those bold, theatrical preachers, somewhat like a bull in a china shop. Seeing him again after a few years, it was great to have the chance to thank him and to catch up on what God was doing in his life.

"Why don't you move back to Minneapolis and come work for me?" Roger asked. "I want to start an international evangelistic organization, and you can help me build and run it." I paused before I responded, remembering the conversations Karen and I had been having recently. We both knew that our time in Sisseton was coming to an end, but we weren't quite sure what was next. Someday we knew we would be going to other nations, but we weren't yet sure what that would look like and when it would happen. *Is this it? Maybe the time is now?* I thought to myself.

"When would you want me to start?" I asked.

"As soon as you can. I want to get started right away."

Karen and I prayed about the opportunity and felt God was saying yes. It was just two months later that we were driving down the highway through Minnesota with our meager belongings inside a small U-Haul trailer. We had just purchased our first house in Minneapolis, a half-mile from where Karen grew up. Somehow, we were able to buy it for two thousand dollars down with a contract-for-deed arrangement.

It felt like this was where we were supposed to be. Everything seemed to fit. We were part of a large, dynamic, congregation, where we enjoyed great worship, and I was just given free rein to build a new ministry focused on global evangelism. Oh, and I received a raise in salary to boot! The church members were excited to see one of their pastors starting an international evangelistic ministry. They started to give generously, so we had excess funds to produce our own glossy magazine. It seemed like every gift I had, along with my experience with the Lundstroms, would be used in this new job. I was on top of the world.

Karen was enjoying our new life too. She loved being back in a metropolitan area with real grocery stores, and she was teaching a fitness class for the women at the church. We just had our second daughter, Lindsay, and were close enough to both sets of our parents to have a bit of support raising our kids. It seemed like everything was turning out perfect. I never would have imagined this season would turn out to be one of the most difficult of our lives.

Another Test

For the first few months, everything seemed to be a dream come true. But then I noticed something seemed a bit off in the leadership of the church. I had no idea why, but there was obvious strife and an underlying spirit of competition among the senior pastors. Roger was telling me all sorts of accusing stories about the other main leader, and I wasn't sure what to believe. He was also acting very paranoid and insecure about his own leadership position in the church. I was still a fairly new and idealistic Christian. Up to this point, I just assumed all good Christians loved each other and got along.

"You can't trust these guys." He would tell me. "They're working to kick me out." He thought there was a brewing conspiracy to oust him from his pastoral position at the church. I wondered if these feelings of mistrust were something he had brought with him from his drug dealing days. I didn't want to believe that Christian leaders could act the way he was describing.

I had never had this experience before and didn't know what to do. My time with Lowell, who was a man of integrity, was rewarding and positive. He didn't badmouth other leaders. He was faithful to his wife and family, and he expressed tremendous faith, even in difficult situations. So, I tried my best to keep building the ministry, scheduling evangelistic campaigns overseas. Excited about international missions, I put my attention into the nations we were planning to go to, like the Philippines, Nigeria, and Kenya. Hoping the older leaders would solve their own problems, I kept myself focused on the future.

Roger continued receiving invitations to preach from around the world, and the opportunities were growing. However, the strife between the two leaders remained. Now both men were vying to get me and the other members of the church staff on their respective side. The spiritual environment became tense and even more toxic. But even in this volatile atmosphere, the Lord was confirming my call to missions.

The international missions trips were always a welcome break. When I got on an airplane, it was with a sigh of relief. Even with all the drama going on at our home church, we were experiencing New Testament style signs and wonders. It was like a different world. Roger would preach to thousands and tens of thousands in the campaigns, and altars were flooded with many people getting saved, healed, and delivered. This was everything I had dreamed about.

But even on these trips, Roger could be a challenge. Several times, when he was about to speak, he couldn't remember what he was going to say. One time in Nigeria, while sitting on stage in front of thousands of people, he leaned over and asked me, "What should I preach?" I found myself giving him sermon notes right there on the spot before he went up to the pulpit. Something was seriously wrong. I still didn't understand his erratic behavior. More and more, it was getting so that Roger was just the face of the ministry. Few knew that it was actually a twenty-five-year-old kid running the show.

When we got home, Roger started acting even more erratic. Sometimes he didn't show up for work. When he did, he displayed dramatic mood swings and even had the occasional red-faced angry rant. He was dangerously overweight and clearly had high blood pressure. I never knew, day by day, what to expect from my boss, and his roller-coaster behavior was now out in the open for the whole church to see. At the same time, to add to the drama, multiple women at the church had accused the other pastor of inappropriate sexual conduct during pastoral counseling sessions.

The work environment became so toxic and challenging that it was finally all coming to a head and could no longer be ignored. Karen and I began to cry out to the Lord. "God, what is going on?" I asked. "You led me here to work with this ministry and called me to the nations. How can I serve leaders who act like this?" I was the youngest on staff and did not have the experience, nor was I equipped, to handle the growing mess now taking over our lives and the church.

Looking for Answers

Karen and I started searching the Scriptures for answers while praying about our church situation. We were only in our mid-twenties, and these were our senior leaders and pastors. How could we, at our age, be the ones to bring correction into this quagmire? It felt like I had been pulled into a swamp and was starting to sink into the muck and mire myself. I needed to hear from the Lord. I needed Him to tell me what to do.

On one occasion God led us to the story of David and Saul. The prophet Samuel anointed David king of Israel while Saul was still on the throne. David was only around fifteen years old at the time and had to wait until he was thirty to become king of Israel. During this time, Saul was hostile. He was tormented by an evil spirit and even tried to kill David on numerous occasions.

God used this period in David's life to him, to see if he would still honor Saul. David passed the test, even risking his own life and reputation, and at the right time was made king. David was a man of integrity. Was God trying to teach me how to honor leadership and walk in integrity, even in difficult situations?

It would be years before I fully understood the answer to this question. But Karen and I felt that we were being tested and needed to honor our leadership while having hearts of integrity. The Lord wasn't just dealing with the leaders; he was also dealing with the motivations of our own hearts.

The whole church was in turmoil, and people were either leaving or feeling pressure to pick sides. I was becoming increasingly frustrated. The other pastor was charming and well liked. The rumors and accusations concerning his alleged immorality were mounting, but no one wanted to confront the man and get mud on their hands. By default, one day at a church leadership meeting, I found myself—one of the youngest members of the church staff—the only one willing to confront the other pastor about his sexual misconduct.

Moral Integrity

The evidence was now very clear there were numerous moral failings, yet he refused to repent or resign. The church kept going downhill with nothing in sight to stop the slide. It was just a few weeks later I discovered what was behind Roger's erratic behavior. Roger had become a drug addict again, but this time it was prescription medication. He had established an elaborate web of prescriptions to get codeine from multiple doctors in the city.

Karen and I were devastated. We were still young Christians, and now our spiritual leaders—men we had both looked up to as pastors, teachers, and role models—had fallen off their pedestals. We felt deeply disappointed and broken.

We needed healing and a break from the chaos. Our own walk with the Lord even felt a bit shaky. We knew we had to go back to original foundations. We needed our own spiritual root system to go deeper than it had been before. This season turned into an important time of spiritual pruning in our lives. We were learning how to handle disappointment by keeping our eyes fixed on Jesus. He never fails or disappoints. Developing intimacy with Him would sustain us for the long run. It was an important lesson we had to learn, because there would be more disappointments and setbacks in the future. We needed to become unshakable.

Integrity Makes You Secure

Sometimes you learn more from mistakes and failures. In this case, they were someone else's. I never wanted to repeat the failures of these leaders I once respected. It was later I found out that lack of moral and financial integrity are the top reasons ministers and missionaries lose their callings. Through the years,

I have watched multiple Christian leaders fall and lose everything. When I mean everything, I don't just mean their ministry and calling. I mean their marriages, families, relationships, and more. Watching what happened with our two pastors, I developed a strong fear of the Lord at a young age. *If talented, even anointed, leaders could fall, what would keep me from that same fate? How could I walk in integrity?*

Billy Graham, Man of Integrity

I started to look around for a role model to follow. Thankfully, I didn't have to look very far. I had come to Christ at a Billy Graham Crusade when I was just fifteen years old, and I recognized him as a man of tremendous integrity. What did Billy Graham do to keep his integrity over all those years? Surely, he was tempted like anyone else. He had plenty of fame, which can easily lead to a man's downfall. His travel schedule took him away from his wife and family for days and weeks at a time. That could open the door for immorality and marriage problems. I discovered that Billy Graham had the same concerns I did, and at age thirty, he made his own covenant with God.

It was back in 1948 that Billy Graham with his young ministry team—Cliff Barrows, Grady Wilson, and George Beverly Shea—met together in Modesto, California, to discuss biblical morality and integrity. Each man had started by making his own list of problems a traveling minister encountered. When they gathered together, they found their lists to be very similar, so they put together a series of resolutions and shared commitments to follow.

Money: Money was the first point on the list. They determined to put in a series of financial accountabilities. One was to take a predetermined salary and turn in all offerings to the ministry headquarters. On a campaign tour, the local cities would oversee and keep the finances separate. Later on, Billy himself put a cap on his yearly salary, which he kept for the rest of his life.

Sexual Immorality: Sexual immorality was the second item on the list. Many evangelists and ministers traveled and spent a lot of time away from their wives and families. The four men all knew the sad stories of their contemporaries who had succumbed to sexual temptation. They made a commitment to avoid any situation that could have the appearance of compromise or garner suspicion. They decided not to travel with, meet privately with, or eat alone with any woman who wasn't their wife. They based this on 2 Timothy 2:22, "Flee the evil desires of youth and pursue righteousness, faith, love and peace, along with those who call on the Lord out of a pure heart."

The Local Church: The consensus was to not critique the local church, but instead to work with local congregations whenever possible. This was to counter what many other evangelists were doing at that time: publicly criticizing local churches instead of striving for unity.

Publicity: They determined not to exaggerate their success and inflate attendance or the number of decisions for Christ. Some evangelists were known for misrepresenting numbers, which often tarnished their reputation. They chose truth instead of pride and dishonesty.

The Modesto Manifesto was never an official document. It was more of an informal agreement between four young men who knew they needed to follow biblical principles for the sake of their own spiritual longevity. They wrote the Modesto Manifesto together so they could hold each other accountable. As the years went by, Billy Graham's ministry would add to and clarify these simple standards, making Billy Graham and his ministry the gold standard for financial and moral integrity in the Christian ministry world.

Karen and I adopted these standards and have chosen to live by them for the rest of our lives. We are thankful for people like Billy Graham, who have modeled a life of integrity. Integrity matters. It's what keeps a person steady and secure for the long journey of life in ministry—and it's what Karen and I wanted more than anything.

God's leading was clear. Now was the time to begin our own ministry. We had spent a number of years serving other leaders, learning many things including how to serve. It developed skill sets beyond our age in marketing, evangelism, event management, fundraising, and church planting.

I put these skills to use by starting a small advertising and consulting company. Evangelists and pastors that I had encountered were now wanting to learn how to build their ministries. I found that I really enjoyed helping them develop their vision and build the appropriate structure to serve it. I was also making more money than I had ever dreamed, many times more than the previous ministries I had worked with. These years were a season of rapid personal growth. I learned marketing, partner development, photography, television, and how to build and run a corperation.

I was visiting Christian music festivals, interviewing artists and speakers for a new TV show I had started. Many of the most popular Christian figures at the time were part of my shows. It was during this season that we moved our family to Colorado Springs. One of my clients, Nicky Cruz, asked if I would help him rebuild his evangelistic ministry. Over the first year in Colorado, we helped build an infrastructure and campaign ministry that would carry him forward in his global evangelistic calling. I found this exciting because we were working with new audiences around America and the world, even inner city gangs.

It was during this season that the Lord began to talk to Karen and I about church planting. We had worked with thousands of churches, been part of the innerworkings of a megachurch, but had never considered church planting ourselves. The Lord eventually led us back to the city where we grew up: Minneapolis, Minnesota, planting a church in one of the roughest and hardest neighborhoods. We used what I knew best which was evangelism to build our first church congregation. Having purchased an old movie theater, we use the space for a Saturday night concert with an altar call. The next morning, on a Sunday, had our first service with those who had come to Christ the night before!

I was soon to find that starting the churches, growing the attendance numbers, and doing evangelism, were the easy parts. Pastoring a rapidly growing congregation and building the systems that make a successful church would be the hard part.

This was a very important and necessary phase for Karen and I. We found ourselves learning so much in the months that followed. We were also building relationships that would last our lifetimes.

God was using this to show me what soon would become a church planting movement in other countries.

Speaking multiple times a week, starting a small church-based Bible college, and still doing evangelistic campaigns forced me into spending large amounts of time studying God's word. I was teaching hundreds of hours, through the entire Bible, and producing training courses on some of the favorite books. I found that I had a deep love and passion to learn God's Word. This was before the internet, so I had thousands of books including hundreds of commentaries. They would be spread out in our home, on the dining room table, on the living room floor, in the bedroom, and of course in my office. The more I studied, the more questions I had. I wanted an answer for every single one.

These years in the early 1980's were not only a great adventure with our young family, but would prepare us for the global responsibilities that would lie ahead. Looking back, it is clear that God was exposing us to as many different aspects of ministry as He could in this formative years.

Chapter 4

Living My Generational Blessing

Growing up, I spent my summers at our family's cabin in the woods of northwest Wisconsin. It was a rustic place without running water, hidden amidst acres of green trees, blue lakes, and gently flowing rivers. The small town of Atlas was only about a mile from our cabin. So, as a boy I would meander down to the general store in the heart of town each morning to buy my daily allotment of candy. Behind the store was one of the many lakes where my friends and I would swim and fish off a rowboat, enjoying warm, lazy summer days—that is, when we weren't taking turns swinging from a rope into the nearby river. Then there were the days we would just wander through the vast woods, looking for adventure or anything that a curious kid might deem dangerous. This is where I felt wild at heart, free to imagine. It was the closest a boy could get to living out the tales of Tom Sawyer or Huckleberry Finn.

What I didn't know at the time was that just a hundred yards away from the little general store, right there on the main street, was a church planted by my very own great-grandfather Axel Anderson. He was one of the famous circuit riding Methodist preachers who traveled in the region, and the town of Atlas was on his circuit. Planted in the early 1900s, the Atlas Methodist Church was once the center of spiritual and community life in the area. As a child growing up, it never occurred to me that this was somehow connected to my family and even my future.

The Methodist Church

Years later, and now married with two children, Karen and I would often go to Atlas on weekends. In the summer of 1988, while vacationing at the rustic cabin, we brought our daughters, Christelle and Lindsay, who were eleven and seven at the time, to the same Atlas general store to buy snacks and their favorite treats. Right next door was the old Methodist church, still standing.

As we walked by the Methodist church, Christelle, curious and looking for an adventure, said, "Let's go in!"

"It's probably not open, but we can check," I replied. As it turned out, the door was unlocked. We looked around first before hesitantly walking inside. The foyer was small, only about twenty by twenty feet. Old black and white photos were mounted on the walls and kept behind glass, telling the history of the church. It felt as though we were in a museum, taking a look back in time. We started studying the pictures, and then Karen noticed an inscription below a photo of the church that read, "Founded by Axel John Anderson." Looking more closely, I found Axel, complete with his thick, dark mustache, smiling face, and bowtie.

Christelle declared, "He has the same name as us!"

"I think he must be your great-great grandfather," Karen answered. This was something I had learned from conversations with my dad, but I had never really investigated the life or ministry of Axel John Anderson. Now, however, I was filled with questions: *Is there a spiritual connection I need to discover? Who was this man? What was he like? What else did he do?* Karen continued, seeming to know more about my family than I did, "He was a circuit rider."

Now our seven year old, Lindsay, was even starting to pay attention. "What's a circuit rider?" she asked.

Karen explained, in language a seven-year-old could understand, "They were preachers who rode horses and traveled America's frontiers, preaching the gospel and bringing revivals." Something deep inside of me stirred. As I continued to look at the different pictures on the walls, one with Axel in what looked like a teen youth group and another of Axel with a choir, I asked myself, *Did he sing? Did he play instruments? Did he write music? Why hadn't I ever looked into my spiritual heritage?*

The Circuit Rider

As soon as Karen, the kids, and I returned to our home in Minneapolis, I went directly to my parents' house. Sitting on the porch with Mom and Dad, notebook in hand, I began to drill them with questions about the spiritual history of Dad's family.

"Dad, why haven't you ever told me more about Axel?" I asked.

Mom was the first to respond, "Your father was only ten years old when Axel died. He never really knew him."

Not satisfied with this answer, I kept probing, "Yeah, but Grandpa Erhard would have known."

A short time later, I visited my grandpa and peppered him with my questions. I also found out my great grandfather's youngest sister had published a family tree with some stories about the Anderson side of the family, which included Axel. Between the conversations with my grandfather and the family tree, I found many of the answers I was looking for. It wasn't too long after I talked with Grandpa Erhard that he died, but not before my sister, Judy, led him to the Lord.

My great-grandfather Axel Anderson was born in Västmanland, Sweden, in 1863. By the time he was 18 years of age, he had become a Swedish Methodist circuit rider, planting his first church in the first year of his ministry.

I learned that circuit riders were preachers and church planters who traveled mostly by horseback. They worked in specific geographic territories, ministering to small towns and organizing congregations. The various towns were on a circuit and would be visited by the circuit rider regularly according to a specified time table. For example, if there were just four towns on a circuit, the preacher would go once a month to each town to preach and hold revival services. Circuit riders were known as rugged, fiery preachers who confronted sin, called for repentance, and moved people to a "verdict." This "verdict" was a public decision to surrender every part of one's life to Jesus. The new converts were then organized into a fellowship of believers that met on a regular basis.

Axel Anderson

Unbeknownst to me, I was following in the footsteps of my circuit riding great-grandfather, Axel. From 1980 to 1990, my life moved incredibly fast. I was on Christian television, planted new churches, and conducted large, international, evangelistic campaigns. It was a decade filled with adventure and global travel. Instead of riding horseback and staying in a local geographic region, however, I would get in a car or an airplane to travel around the world.

While I was discovering my spiritual heritage, a church in Minneapolis we planted in 1983 was growing rapidly. It met in an old movie theater and used the adjoining retail space for Sunday school rooms. In just the first year of the church plant, 2,260 people came to Christ. Over the following years, between pastoring and speaking at evangelistic campaigns, I preached over three thousand messages. I loved the Word of God, and I loved to preach. It seemed like I was doing what I was designed by God to do.

I had no idea that my great-grandfather had done a similar thing in his generation. Although limited in his ability to travel, he preached, planted churches, and gave up everything for missions. *Was there a generational connection, call, or blessing being passed down?* Many of the locations where circuit riders ministered were in rural areas and rugged wilderness. Axel started in south-central Sweden, where there are multitudes of lakes and rivers. He traveled on horseback and used a small boat to move up and down the waterways. All this rowing and paddling gave Axel strong shoulders and arms. He had to be physically tough but spiritually sensitive.

Late in his life, Axel wrote about his early experiences in his diary:

> *Sixty-two years ago today I came into the world at Hogfors Bruk in Västmanland, Sweden. At the age of eleven I undertook the huge task of reading the entire Bible, which I did that winter. I recommend that healthy task to every young man and woman."*

In June of 1886, I left my homeland and journeyed to America. On the tenth of July I arrived at Abbotsford, Wisconsin. At first I worked for the railroad on the workdays and ministered on the weekends. Later, I began to minister full-time.

My fiancee, Carolina Christina Pollock, arrived in the spring of 1887. We were married on February 4, 1888, and we then moved to Escanaba, Michigan. Three years later, we returned to Wisconsin when I was appointed to the Prentice Circuit.

Here I found the opportunity to which God had called me. Here I found enough work to satisfy my ambition. I had eleven preaching places in my circuit. I organized three new congregations: Stevens Point, Anhurst/Sheridan, and Wausau.

World War I

Now that I knew a bit about more about Axel, I focused on questioning my Dad. "Why didn't Grandpa Erhard ever talk about Axel? And why didn't he ever go to church?" I could tell this was an awkward subject for my Dad. He was partially choked up as he began to tell me a story I had never heard before.

"Your grandfather Erhard fought in the First World War on the Western Front. He was in the trenches engaged in hand-to-hand combat, day after day. He slept in the mud, sometimes next to dead bodies. He watched many of his friends die. During this terrible season of his life, he began to lose perspective."

My father paused to wipe his eyes and then continued the story: "One time, while in the trenches on the Western front, his whole unit was told to move and carry all their equipment to a new location. Upon arriving in the new trench, they realized they had left behind the tripod for the machine gun. Erhard was assigned to go back and get it. While he was retrieving the tripod, his whole unit was bombed. He quickly ran back, only to find his dead friends and their body parts laying everywhere. From that day on, his perspective on life changed. Later in the war, he was hit with mustard gas. He spent nine months recovering in a French hospital and almost died. He wasn't married yet, and of course, I hadn't been born, but I was told that he came back from the war a different man. He doubted God's existence and stayed away from church completely."

Mom then jumped into the conversation. "Your grandfather then met a beautiful, Christian woman named Ellyn. She loved the Lord and helped restore Erhard's faith. After they were married, she became pregnant with your father. They were a happy family and had gone back to participating in church life. Then your grandmother Ellyn suddenly became sick with cancer, and it quickly spread through her organs. The doctors in that era could do very little other than physically cut out the cancer. She received several brutal operations, which left her crippled. The cancer soon took her life. She died when your father was only eight years old. Erhard couldn't handle losing his wife that way and began to drink, becoming a full-on alcoholic. He drank for more than fifty years and didn't come back to the Lord until just before his death. That was when you witnessed to him and then your sister Judy prayed with him the next day."

My mom paused briefly and then continued, "During the years after Ellyn's death, your father and grandfather wandered from one city to another, and Erhard started business after business. Every one failed because he lived intoxicated. Many times, as a young boy or teenager, your father would have to go into a bar late at night to pull Erhard out and bring him home."

My father then spoke, "Your grandfather was a brilliant man. Several of the businesses he started were hugely successful. He just couldn't maintain them while drinking."

A picture was now forming in my mind. Axel the circuit rider lived a dynamic Christian life, but the enemy had a plan to cut off the generational blessing, starting with my grandfather. The blessing did not get restored in my family until I came to Christ and led my own father back to the Lord. Now all of the random conversations I had with my Grandpa Erhard as a boy started to make sense. One time, when I was thirteen years old, he took me up into the attic and pulled out some artifacts from the First World War. There was a German helmet with a point on top and a sword, both presumably from an enemy that was either killed or captured. As a young boy, I was captivated by the stories and the war paraphernalia.

Grandfather never wanted to talk much about this time in his life, but I can remember him telling me the Germans really weren't bad guys. He said that they were just like us, but they were forced to fight. He continued telling me that he had to kill them, because that was his duty. I now knew why Grandfather walked away from God after the war. He was paralyzed by guilt. His Christian upbringing taught him to be loving and kind, but he was forced in war to do things he felt were wrong.

I had flashbacks to the times I would see my grandfather after he drank a bottle of wine. He would be laughing and joking. I thought he was just being silly, and I didn't take him too seriously. But now I understood that this was how he found temporary relief from the weight of his guilt. The true Erhard Anderson was a joy-filled, lighthearted, and kind man, just like his father, Axel. I could picture what the reunion must have been like in heaven when the two men met, completely restored in the presence of Jesus, free from sin and guilt. No doubt they were laughing and singing together.

Now, I was even more determined to study the spiritual legacy and blessing in my family, to learn where I fit and to make sure it would pass down to my children and grandchildren. I had read in the Bible about blessings being passed down generationally. *Was there a blessing or calling my family line was meant to receive and carry?* I wanted to find out.

Multi-Generational Callings

I wanted to learn everything I could about how circuit riders lived. Why were they so effective? They were part of a dynamic move of God, carrying the Second Great Awakening across America's frontiers. I wanted to follow the same pattern and sensed I somehow had a spiritual inheritance in the unfolding storyline. Understanding this could give me the keys to seeing a move of God in my lifetime and then in my children and grandchildren.

Circuit riders lived on almost nothing, earning just a few dollars a year from the Methodist denomination and receiving periodic gifts of food from their congregations. Often, they lived in the raw wilderness, studying the Bible and preparing for their sermons as they rode horseback. They would arrive at their ministry destinations exhausted, saddle-sore, and with no guarantee of housing for the night. They had to be tough and fully committed to what they were doing. So did their families, who not only moved on a regular basis, but often served as the ministry staff. They had to learn to live on very little, sometimes getting paid with chickens, eggs, or other farm produce.

My great-grandparents Axel and Carolina lived this hard life with great joy. They traveled with their nine children to places like Holland, Marquette, and Escanaba, Michigan; Stevens Point, Sheridan, Trade Lake, Atlas, and Wausau, Wisconsin; and Litchfield, Willmar, Kandiyohi, and Minneapolis, Minnesota. Those who knew them when they were alive remembered their love of music, singing, dancing, and nature.

The life of a circuit rider was hard. Half of these ministers died before the age of thirty-three. One of the rules of the denomination was that circuit rider families could only stay in one region for two years at a maximum. This must have been challenging for my great-grandparents with their large family of nine children.

After the discovery of my circuit rider grandfather, Karen and I often had discussions about this legacy. It gave me lots to think about. *What was God's original purpose and design for family? How do I walk in the blessing of the Lord in my family? How do I pass this blessing down to my children and grandchildren?* This was eternal thinking, kingdom thinking.

The Family is Meant to Rule

We were discovering for the first time God's multi-generational relationship with his creation of man and woman. It was clear that everything started with the family, and the family had been given an assignment: to be fruitful, to increase, to fill, to subdue, and to rule. "So God created mankind in his own image, in the image of God he created them; male and female he created them. God blessed them and said to them, 'Be fruitful and increase in number; fill the earth and subdue it. Rule over the fish in the sea and the birds in the sky and over every living creature that moves on the ground'" (Genesis 1:27–28). This truth now seemed so obvious. How could we have ever missed it? This is the role of the family on earth. The family is meant to advance God's Kingdom on earth.

> **Be Fruitful:** The family is meant to prosper and bear "fruit." Every human being is part of a family, and the family core to all the other spheres of society. It's out of a healthy family that a person is launched to influence and shape their surrounding culture and spheres of society.

> **Increase:** The family is meant to get larger and more numerous. Husbands and wives having children is part of God's divine plan to advance His kingdom on earth.

> **Fill:** Through the family, we are meant to take over. As time goes on, there should be greater influence through the family, not less.

> **Subdue:** The family is not meant to take a passive role on earth. It should be the first sphere of society that takes action to shape the rest of society. This might sound militant, but it fits into the idea of advancing heaven on earth.

> **Rule:** The first form of government God established was the family. Family is central and key to all other forms of rule and government. Other forms of government should not rule over the first form of government, the family.

Generational Blessings and Callings

"'He is the God of Abraham, Isaac and Jacob….' Genealogies are everywhere in the Bible," I explained to Karen. "Blessings and curses are passed down through generations!"

"How about callings?" Karen asked. She was bringing up an important question: Are there really multi-generational callings?

From the beginning of our marriage, we learned to start the day together with our Bibles and prayer, realizing the most powerful thing we could do as husband and wife was to pray in agreement over our family. During these times, we would pray for our children, that they would follow God's direction and walk in His blessing. A parent's greatest joy is seeing their children and grandchildren walk with the Lord and to continue the generational blessing in their own lives.

I couldn't get Karen's question out of my mind. *Are there really multi-generational callings?* In biblical terms, Axel Anderson's ministry was apostolic, not in the sense of the original apostles, but as a forerunner and pioneer, blazing trails for others to follow. When Jesus left the earth, He gave five gifts to the church—five roles to equip and lead His people—and the first one listed is that of an apostle (Ephesians 4:11–13).

When I was young, I used to like to watch the TV program *Star Trek.* Every show would open with the same words: "To boldly go where no man has gone before!" Karen used to make fun of me when I watched this show. She thought it was dorky with all of its strange characters. What intrigued me the most was finding someplace where no person had been before, doing something no one had tried, blazing a new trail.

As a young boy in the woods of Wisconsin near my parents' cabin, I would intentionally take my machete and go to the most remote portion of the forest where my mother warned me not to go. She was afraid I would get lost in the thousands of acres. What she didn't understand was, that was my intent. I wanted to walk somewhere nobody had ever walked before. I wanted to find a new river or new lake, or discover some animal no one knew was there. I was in it for the adventure.

If you're like me, you've had very little teaching on what the ministry of the apostle looks like or what an apostolic anointing entails. Jesus gave five ministry gifts to the church in Ephesians 4:11–13: apostle, prophet, evangelist, pastor, and teacher. What I thought was just my personality as a young boy—the desire to be a pioneer—I now realize is part of my ministry gifting. I have always carried an apostolic anointing in some way.

The Methodist circuit riders are clear examples of apostolic pioneers. My great-grandfather Axel did this in both Scandinavia and the northern Midwest states of America. It was becoming clear that this was a calling on me and our family line. Besides the traditional church or missionary calling, we were meant to be pioneers in every sphere of life. The family, education, economics, government, celebration, and media spheres all need missional apostles to reach people with the gospel and bring transformation. I felt the Lord was restoring in me something that had actually been lost for a few generations. I was discovering that's God calling on my life was connected to the past. This made me wonder what the generations following me were meant to accomplish on this earth.

Now it was starting to make sense. The callings from one generation to the next were continual, even though they might look different. My own ministry was similar to the ministry of Axel Anderson, only in a different generation and using different methods. But, as a Methodist circuit rider, he was a pioneer.

I had more questions than answers. *What kind of covenants did my great-grandfather Axel cut with God? He was a man of prayer, but what did he ask for? Did he pray for his grandchildren and great-grandchildren? Did he ask for geographic areas of the world?*

Karen and I didn't see it at the time, but during this season, we went from just doing ministry work to developing movements that would find a life of their own, perhaps extending into multi-generational callings. Of course, the first place that this had to happen was in our own family.

Chapter 5

Being Bold

During the 1980s, the churches Karen and I planted in the United States grew rapidly, particularly the one in the inner city of Minneapolis. Though still a very young congregation, it had been missional from the first day. The church began with an evangelistic outreach where seventy-two people came to Christ. Those seventy-two constituted ninety percent of those in attendance for the first official church service.

India:

After one of our Sunday morning services, a man walked up to me and introduced himself as Harley. He explained that he was a missionary to India who worked primarily in Andhra Pradesh, a state in the south of the country. He invited me to come to India and preach in one of the villages where he was doing his work. Little did I know Harley's invitation would be the turning point that would lead Karen and me into extensive evangelism, church planting, and mercy work for years to come.

In the months that followed, I challenged my nephew, Scott, and our church youth leader, Eric, to get together with Harley and take a trip to India to "spy out the land." They were both students at Northwestern Bible College, but up until that point they hadn't had any real missions experience.

In just a matter of weeks, Scott and Eric were on a plane to India. Once there, they found themselves in the middle of a culture not all that different from the culture Jesus knew. Across thousands of small villages, most of the people in India lived relatively simple lives—and they were very open to the message of Jesus. The most exciting part was how quickly they believed for physical healings and miracles.

"Mark! You won't believe what's happening!" It was Scott on the other end of the phone, calling from India. Somehow, he managed to find a phone that could make an international call. "This country is wide open," he continued. "People are so hungry! Why don't we do a major evangelistic campaign? We could organize it, and you could be the evangelist." While he was talking, I felt confirmation from the Holy Spirit and excitement about the potential for a move of God in a foreign country.

In the following weeks, everything happened rapidly. We found ourselves organizing a major evangelistic event in the city of Guntur. I found that Scott had a gift for making friends in a foreign country and a natural talent for organization. In a short amount of time, he had secured campaign grounds that would hold fifty thousand people, found the appropriate sound system, set up the advertising, and made connections with top officials in the area. There was so much excitement in the city of Guntur that the national press was going to send reporters to cover the campaign.

Soon, I was on a flight to India. I landed in Hyderabad and met Scott and our Indian coordinator, Chandra Bose. We then made the long drive southeast to the city of Guntur. They had arranged for me to stay in a small home not far from the campaign grounds.

While driving into Guntur, I could see the posters for our campaign plastered everywhere. It felt odd because my picture was on the poster, making it seem that I was something of a celebrity. As we entered the guest house, I could see Scott and Bose were bubbling over with excitement about what was happening in the city of Guntur. "Mark! Everybody is talking about this campaign! All the major newspapers in the country are represented here, and you're scheduled to meet them tomorrow." Bose jumped in, "City officials and even the inspector general for South India will be in attendance!" I could feel their excitement, but after traveling for forty-five hours, I needed to find a bed and get some rest.

Signs and Wonders

This was October of 1984. The rainy season was over, but you could still feel the humidity in the air. The morning of the first day of our eight day campaign, I rode with Scott and Bose out to the grounds to see the stage and sound system. We drove onto a huge dusty field in the middle of town. I couldn't help but think, "How are we going to fill this?" I could see at the other end of the field the large, crudely built stage, erected on stilts with uneven boards two meters above the ground so that everyone on the field would be able to see. Electric blackouts were commonplace, so they had a generator sitting behind the stage in case the power went out. All around the field were crooked poles with mounted lights and primitive wire running from one pole to the next. There were sections roped off so that men and women in attendance could be separated.

Bose explained what would probably happen with the evening crowds, "The first night will have fewer people, but when they hear the message and see the miracles, the crowds will grow dramatically night after night." As he predicted, the first night saw only about three thousand in attendance. There was an hour of singing first, and then I began telling stories about Jesus. A translator stood next to me, communicating to the people in the local language of Telugu.

When I got to the parts where Jesus healed the sick, I was startled at how the people in the crowd began to respond. The same thing happened as I talked about Jesus casting out devils. People would shriek and sometimes hit the ground and roll. It was clear that the Word of God had power, and people were receiving these stories by faith. In the following minutes, people who had been touched physically began to line up along each side of the stage. I whispered to the translator, "What are they doing?"

He responded, *"They've been healed, and they want to tell their story."*

I began to invite people up, one-by-one. *"As you were talking, I was healed of my stomach pain!"* one person said.

"I couldn't walk on my right leg, but now it's normal!" said another.

"I couldn't see, but now I can see everything!"

As each person testified, the faith in the crowd grew. More and more people began having dramatic encounters with the Lord. My preaching now became more direct. I began to address demonic strongholds in people's lives, and I confronted sickness and disease directly. For the next couple of hours, the Lord touched hundreds of people in miraculous ways, setting them free, healing their bodies, and performing miracles.

When the time came for the altar call, it seemed as though everyone was ready to pray with me. I led the three thousand who gathered that night in a prayer of repentance, surrender, and confession of Christ's lordship. I could see people weeping as they were filled with the Holy Spirit.

As Bose had predicted, on the second night the crowd more than doubled in size. If this trend continued, by the end of the eight days this entire field would be packed. Reporters were already sending stories off to their newspapers, telling what was happening. Our entire team felt a genuine excitement about the move of the Holy Spirit we were seeing and what it could mean for the region in the months ahead.

Emergency:

As I lay down late that night, I was exhausted but deeply grateful to the Lord for what He was doing. I also felt excitement about what could happen in the next few days. "Thank you, Jesus, for allowing me to be a part of this awakening," I prayed.

It was only six in the morning when I heard a pounding knock on my bedroom door. I rolled over and said, "Go away!" I couldn't believe that somebody would wake me up after just a few hours of sleep, but the pounding continued. My eyes half open, I dragged myself out of bed and walked to the door. "What do you want?" I asked. On the other side of the door was Bose.

"I have to talk to you! It's an emergency!" he said. I hurriedly threw my clothes on and opened the door. "The country is beginning to riot!" he exclaimed. "The Prime Minister Indira Gandhi has been assassinated. Her Sikh guards shot her, and now a radical Hindu element is moving into the streets and rioting all across the country!" We were soon joined by Scott, and we all went to prayer, asking the Lord what we should do. We knew we couldn't continue with our evangelistic campaign or we would risk endangering the people.

Outside, things were getting worse by the minute. Radicals were burning down stores with people still inside. Buses packed with people were being stopped and set on fire. Roads were being blocked with logs, and people were getting pulled out of their cars and beaten up. Westerners in the country were being warned to leave.

We knew we had to get out to the airport that night, so we arranged for a four-wheel drive car and, under the cover of darkness, traveled outside of the city to catch the first morning flight. Even while traveling to the airport, we had to navigate the blocked streets and drive over logs laid across, the road. The next morning we were able to catch a flight to the major airport, get a connection, and fly out of the country.

These events moved so quickly, I didn't have time to process what was happening. Sitting on the plane as we flew out of India, I spoke to the Lord, "I don't understand. You led us to this city. You blessed our first two nights with a strong presence of Your Spirit. We saw signs and wonders alongside the preaching of Your Word, and now we're fleeing the country. Did we miss something?"

7 Times Greater:

Disappointed, I came home to the church we had just started in Minneapolis. It was a young and vibrant congregation, and people were waiting for us to come home with great praise reports. Many had given for this outreach, some of them sacrificially. What would I tell them?

I arrived home on a Friday, so I had a little time to regroup before the Sunday service. Though I was still jet lagged, Karen and I went to the Lord for more clarity. On Saturday morning, after a time of worship, we prayed and did our best to enter into the presence of the Lord. It was during this time that God led me to Deuteronomy 28. Verse 7 seemed to jump off the page: "The LORD will grant that the enemies who rise up against you will be defeated before you. They will come at you from one direction but flee from you in seven." I began to understand on a much deeper level that we have an enemy and that he does rise up against us. However, if we remain in faith, he'll come at us from one direction but have to flee in seven.

God makes it clear there is a battle and we have a very real enemy. There is an ebb and flow in a spiritual battle just as there is in an earthly battle. It was then that an idea came to my mind: What if we went back to India as soon as possible and planned an outreach many times larger? I pulled out a map and began to search for the cities near Guntur. Not too far away was a larger city called Vijayawada.

The next morning, I went into the pulpit, telling the story of what happened in Guntur but boldly proclaiming, "We're going to go back, and it will be seven times more effective!" To my delight, this large group of young believers got excited, and we even took up the first offering toward our next outreach.

Back to India

Just a few months later, we made our way back to India to conduct a campaign in the large city of Vijayawada. Once again, Scott and Bose met us at the airport. After a warm embrace, we jumped in the car and made our way to the heart of the city. Driving along,

I could see many temples dedicated to the gods of Hinduism. Vijayawada is the city where the Beatles famously traveled in their search for truth. Many hippies during the '60s made their way to this city for a spiritual pilgrimage. I was thinking to myself that it would be just like God to make Himself known in a city like this.

Before driving me to my guest quarters, Scott wanted to show me the campaign grounds. Driving up, I could see that it was massive, much larger than the one in Guntur. The stage was higher and about twice the size of the last one. The speakers were mounted on poles that put them eighty feet in the air. The city was saturated with advertisements, and there were hundreds of thousands of flyers being passed out. Everything was prepared for God to do seven times as much!

The campaign began on a Sunday night with about four thousand people. God's presence was tangible in our midst, and just like before, people were being delivered and healed while I was speaking. Many came to the stage testifying to what God had done in their lives. Once again, it seemed like everyone in attendance surrendered their life to Christ. The next day, the numbers surged to about seven thousand. Momentum was building, and the word was getting out across the city.

We were also getting kickback from local officials who were Hindu. They were doing their best to shut us down. They took all our team members' passports and threatened to kick us out of the country. Fortunately, we had the inspector general of South India, one of the highest officials in the land, on our board. Each time we had a problem, he was able to resolve it with a simple phone call.

Boldness

On the morning of the third day, I called the staff together and said, "Let's be especially alert and prayerful today. Remember what happened in Guntur on the third day!" I spent much of the day praying and studying the Word, getting clarity from the Lord on what He wanted me to say. I was led to 1 Corinthians 12, where Paul lists gifts of the Spirit. I couldn't help but wonder, *Does God have something in mind for tonight that will dramatically show His power?* Perhaps the Lord was planning a direct response to what the enemy did in Gunter on the third day.

I could hear our staff leaving the house at about five o'clock p.m. to go out to the campaign grounds. My vehicle was scheduled to leave about two hours later. Just before seven, I walked out of the guest house and looked up. I could see a dark and massive storm moving into the city. In the distance, I could see sheets of rain coming down. The wind was already starting to blow. The storm was close. I thought to myself, *Oh no! This will shut down the whole evening! This can't happen.*

I jumped in the car and told the driver to get me to the campaign grounds as quickly as possible. He drove as fast as he could through the city, honking his horn the whole way. As we pulled onto the grounds, I could see there were ten thousand people or more there, all stirring, aware that a storm was coming.

The driver pulled up alongside the stage, where Bose was standing with the translator. I quickly got out of the car, laid my hands on the translator, and began to pray, "Lord, give us boldness tonight to declare your Word." I had already felt a unique anointing to believe God for great things. Looking back, I now know this was the special gift of faith that Paul talked about (1 Corinthians 12:9;

13:2). We ran up on the stage and grabbed the mics. I looked out at the crowd and could see people beginning to leave to find shelter from the rain. I told them, "Stop! Don't go anywhere!" Then, while looking at the rain clouds, I declared, "Rain, stop!" The storm was just beginning to make its way over the field, but when it got to the edge, the clouds split and went around us on each side before coming back together behind us. The area above us was left open with no rain. It stayed this way for several hours until the final altar call was finished. Everyone in attendance could see what was happening, and they knew it was supernatural. God had indeed performed a miracle, demonstrating His power for all to see.

The next day, word about what happened spread through the whole city. My staff told me that people were buzzing, talking about what God had done. I didn't know how real this was until I tried to go for a walk. I had just taken a few steps from my guest house when people saw me and began to press on me from every side for prayer. Later, I thought I could sneak out in the back seat of a car. When we made it to the first intersection, people surrounded the car, reaching through the open windows with their young children so they might be blessed. The whole intersection was packed with people clamoring for prayer. The hunger throughout the city was palpable.

When I arrived at the campaign grounds that night, the field was packed. It was clear that we were in the middle of a significant move of God. Evening turned to night, and after the formal gathering was done, people lined up by the thousands to receive prayer. There were so many people being delivered, so many healings and creative miracles, that we couldn't document them all. We had already recorded more than forty thousand decisions for Christ! As I finally made my way to bed in the early hours of the morning, I couldn't help but wonder what God would do next.

It's a Miracle!

The next afternoon, I was with hundreds of pastors in a tent doing leadership training. Having watched what had been happening during the week, they were asking questions, one after another, about how deliverance and healing works. This went on for several hours, and I was exhausted. All I could think about was how to get back to the guest house and take a nap. I had my driver pull up to the back of the tent with his car, and I walked as quickly as I could, but before I could get into the car, one of our staff members ran up to me and said, "Pastor! Pastor! Before you leave please pray for this woman and her son." When I turned my head, I saw a woman with a little boy standing by the edge of the building.

I said, "Why don't you just have them come tonight to receive prayer?"

The worker answered, "Pastor, she's been here all day. She's waited seven hours for you to pray for her son."

I couldn't help but think about the Bible stories where people would wait for Jesus so I said, "Okay, bring them over here quickly."

Through a translator, I asked the woman what was wrong with her son. She replied, "He has no pupils." At that moment, I looked down and saw that she was right; he had no pupils in his eyes. I thought to myself, *This would take a creative miracle from God.* Before I could even pray, the pastors came out of the leaders' meeting and quickly surrounded us. They stared curiously as I prayed for this baby boy. I asked God to do a miracle and restore the pupils in his eyes. Then, I jumped in the car, got back to the guest house, and collapsed on my bed.

That night, the crowd was even larger. The evening was filled with the supernatural, and many thousands more came to Christ. I got to bed at three in the morning, but I was awakened a few hours later by someone pounding on my door. I heard a voice saying, "Did you hear?! Did you hear?!"

Half awake, I stumbled to the door and said, "What happened?"

The voice replied, "They boy that you prayed for—he's healed!"

Still behind the closed door, I replied, "What boy?"

"The boy with no pupils! He now has pupils in his eyes!"

I cracked open the door to see who I was talking to and found one of our senior campaign workers. When he saw me, he continued, "The word is spreading throughout the city—even out into the countryside. Everyone is talking about the miracle!" I closed the door and made my way back to the bed, tired but grateful for all that the Lord was doing.

That night, the mother and little boy, now with pupils in his eyes, joined me on stage. The campaign grounds were packed with people as far as I could see. As the mother shared her testimony, people began to clap and cheer. I couldn't help but think how much this Hindu city had changed in just a few short days. By the end of the week, ninety-six thousand people—more than fourteen percent of the city's population—had come to Christ! The enemy had tried to shut us down, but he ended up fleeing in seven directions. This was a principle I would remember for the rest of my life in ministry.

Chapter 6

From Some to All

Our missions work in the United States and abroad was growing rapidly. God had opened doors into new countries all around the world, and we began to expand our work into church planting, education, and medical care. It was during this season that I met someone who would change the course of my life in dramatic ways. In 1990, I invited Loren Cunningham, the co-founder of Youth With A Mission (YWAM), to speak at a small conference we were holding. I knew a little bit about him from reading his book *Is That Really You, God?* I had also met a few "YWAMers," as they're called, on various mission fields around the world. Often, they were groups of young people who were on an outreach assignment as part of Discipleship Training School (DTS).

Meeting Loren

One of my staff picked up Loren at the Minneapolis-Saint Paul International Airport and drove him to our conference location. It was now time for the evening meal, so he and I went out to a local restaurant and began to talk. Loren had a wonderfully inviting demeanor, and he seemed to have a story ready for any topic that came up. As we sat down to order our meal, the conversation moved to what was happening in various parts of the world. To my surprise, he knew a little bit about me and what we were doing in India. "It sounds like you've been doing some exciting things in India. I remember when I first went there many years ago," he said. He then described what India was like in the 1960s. I was struck by how knowledgeable he was.

"God has allowed us to learn a lot in India, particularly how to evangelize the younger generation and then move them into long-term discipleship," I said. "Church planting movements and K–6 schools are really key."

Loren perked up. "Tell me more about that!"

"We learned that we can use the arts, entertainment, sports, and media to get the attention of young people. This, along with signs and wonders, draws those in any city or village. Then, the follow-through has to be relevant, so we start what we call 'Neighborhood Centers.' These are seven-day-a-week facilities that meet the needs of the people," I elaborated. I now had Loren's interest, and he began to share with me a story about a divine encounter he and Bill Bright had in 1975 about discipling nations. Our conversation moved seamlessly from the restaurant to the hotel where Loren was staying. We talked all through the night and went back to the same restaurant for breakfast. What turned out to be twelve hours of conversation felt like it took only a few minutes. Neither of us had slept, but we didn't care, because we were talking about our favorite subject: how to see Christ revealed in the nations. A bond began that day that

I didn't fully understand YWAM, but I liked Loren and what he was saying. Immediately I thought, *I have to tell Karen!* She was already aware that we had spent the night talking because I had called to tell her I wasn't coming back to our hotel room. I drove our Plymouth van to our hotel, picked her up, and parked in a nearby church parking lot. I had to tell her right away what I was feeling, "Talking with Loren, it was like I had known him my whole life. He's like a spiritual father that I never had. There's some kind of divine connection between us."

Karen, in her usual, thoughtful way responded, "Well, you've really needed somebody older that you could look up to and who could speak into your life."

"Karen, I really think a change is coming. Maybe we are supposed to join YWAM."

"Don't they have to raise their own support?" she responded. "What about the church and all of our global missions projects?"

"I don't know. I just sense a change is coming. Let's ask the Lord and commit all of our ways to Him," I proposed. Then, as we had done some many times before, we joined hands and prayed: "Lord, everything we have is yours, including our future. Show us Your will. We will do whatever you say." Though there were dozens of unanswered questions, we both felt God's peace and a new excitement about what might lie ahead.

A few days later, back in the church office in Minneapolis, I sat down with Barb Livingston to share with her what had happened over the weekend. Barb and her husband, Frank, were members of our church plant. Some years earlier, Barb had become my secretary and then the church administrator. The two of them had given their lives to the Lord back during the Jesus Movement. Coming out of the hippie lifestyle, the two of them knew what it was to follow a new vision.

"Barb, I had an incredible experience with Loren Cunningham," I told her. I then spent the next hour and a half relaying the conversation to her. I also shared what Karen and I were feeling about YWAM.

Barb listened carefully and asked the same question that Karen had: "Don't YWAMers have to raise their own support?" Then she started thinking through the implications of what I was telling her, and she had more questions: "Can you be a pastor and a YWAMer? What about the international ministry? What would you do with that?"

In the weeks that followed, the Lord began to make clear to all of us that a change was coming. It would involve turning the church over to new leadership. Barb and Frank committed to go with Karen and me as God led us in this new direction.

Joining YWAM

Even though I had already been in ministry and global missions for 13 years, it was made clear to me by other YWAMers that, in order to join "the mission," as they called it, I had to complete a DTS (Discipleship Training School) program. This would mean twelve weeks of classroom study followed by an outreach.

By this time, I was talking to Loren regularly and working on global missions strategies, even though I wasn't an official YWAMer yet. He suggested that I do my DTS in northwest Montana at a base just southwest of Kalispell. Karen and I didn't know one base from another but thought Montana sounded nice. After all, the base was right next to a national park. We began getting ready for the move to YWAM. I turned over the church to new leadership. We began raising personal financial support, then packed our family up and moved to the base in Lakeside, Montana.

We moved into what seemed like little motel rooms, except the walls were more like wooden panels than true walls—so thin we could hear the conversations taking place in each room down the hall. Most of the other students seemed to be new Christians or people who had come with lots of problems they needed to figure out.

For almost two decades, God had me on a journey, showing me how to win and disciple the younger generation. With my marketing background, I was always thinking about how to package the message of the gospel to various demographic groups, particularly teens and pre-teens (the age when most people come to Christ). We had successfully developed strategies with music, drama, sports, and creative media to reach hundreds of thousands around the globe. Now, I felt it was time to take this strategy to a whole other level—and YWAM seemed to be the perfect missions movement to host what I had on my mind.

During this time, I came to realize that YWAM was one of the most internationally dispersed organizations in the world, operating in nearly every country around the globe, with bases in most of them. With thousands of self-funded staff, there was a seemingly endless supply of workers who could be trained and deployed just about anywhere. The potential for a missions strategy that could be multiplied was exciting.

Starting a Base

It was during these days that God began to crystalize a new movement in my heart: raising up evangelistic teams that were designed around arts, entertainment, sports, and media to work year-round in locations all around the world. These groups could do tours, much like famous bands do, and be advertised in the secular media. This would move us away from the crusade framework that leaned so heavily on local churches.

When we finished our DTS training, Karen and I needed a place to operate. In YWAM, that means that you need a base, but where should we go? During a time of prayer, God began to stir in my heart the area in Wisconsin where my parents had a cabin, an area where I spent my summers as a young boy. I began to ask around and look for a suitable property. One of the locals told me about a lodge and some buildings that had been built by some investors to be part of an eighteen-hole golf course and resort. We found out that the property was only five miles from my parents' cabin, in the middle of 2,800 acres of beautiful rolling hills with plenty of oak trees and four lakes. As we drove onto the property with the owners, we could see where the greens had been cut for the golf course, though now with grass had grown up to our knees. Going around a bend on a dirt road, we saw a beautiful cedar lodge that had been sitting unused for several years. The owners told us that the golf course never opened up because they ran out of money before it was finished. After we explored the property some, they drove us to a partially built house. It was to be the first of many to be built about a mile from the lodge.

As it turned out, the current owners had bought the land for the oak trees, which were more valuable than a golf course. They said they would sell us the 80-acres where the lodge was located if they could keep the rights to the oak trees, harvesting some of them every few years as they were ready to be cut. It seemed like a perfect deal for what we planned to do with the property. I thought to myself, *I can finish building that house they started, and my family could live there!* Little did I know how difficult it was all going to be. I had never built a house, much less one in the middle of the woods with no access to sewer or water. We signed the deal and were on our way to start our first base!

Somehow I managed to convince Karen and our five children at the time, that we should move to Wisconsin and live on our new base. Barb and Frank also decided to join us. But before we could all move up there, I needed to get the house and lodge ready. I found a retired contractor to work with me on these projects. What seemed at first to be a simple thing became a massive project. I had never gutted and rebuilt a house that had been left unfinished and abandoned for seven years in the woods, nor did I have experience repairing anything like a lodge with collapsed roofs.

Barb and Frank's son, Aaron, was there with me to help, and he loved every minute of it. It was the sort of great adventure every teenager is looking for. He spent his day with construction subs and his free time hunting everything that moved. When the house was ready—really half-finished—our family of seven alongside and Barb, Frank, Katie, and Aaron all moved into the house. We still had no running water, though. My attempts at drilling a well were all unsuccessful. So while we were living in the house, I dug a seven-foot ditch through the woods, three-quarters of a mile long, to reach the main water supply at the lodge. At the same time, I poured the front steps, completed the heating system, and installed the windows in the porch. The floors were still plywood, and some of the walls were unfinished, but we moved in the kitchen appliances and made a home of the place.

The YWAM dream had now begun! We were pioneering a base, starting schools, and building what would become a major evangelistic ministry, while constructing buildings, clearing trees, hauling in gravel for the roads, and of course plowing the six feet of snow that fell each winter.

We were all still traveling back to Minneapolis on the weekends so I could preach at the church services and help the young leaders who had taken over the leadership of the congregation. Often our family of seven would pile into our van early Sunday morning, sometimes with Aaron sitting on the floor, drive an hour and half to the church, conduct the two services, have staff meetings, and then head back in the evening, arriving home in the dark.

Impact World Tour

A new evangelistic ministry in YWAM was starting to emerge. We would call our campaigns Impact Word Tours, or IWT. Our teams would use some area of arts, entertainment, or sports (even extreme sports) to present the gospel. Our two families were the only staff, but we still managed to begin the work of writing the campaign manuals, creating promotional materials, and assembling the first teams. All of it was being done with no real income or office, which meant we were taking a major step backward in finances, staffing, facilities, and just about every other area. But we were pioneering!

I spent my days driving across the Midwest, meeting with pastors and trying to open up their cities for the Impact World Tour. It wasn't an easy thing to market, but several small towns agreed to host the tour. One of them was Spooner, Wisconsin, which later turned to be our first IWT city.

It was now 1993 and, by this time, I had begun to form some evangelistic teams. Island Breeze was an established ministry in YWAM that did cultural performances with elements of a Hawaiian luau. They had never successfully done evangelism with their shows, but I was convinced the performance could not only draw a crowd but also reach people for Christ. Another team called Team Xtreme was just beginning to form and would be built around strength feats and sports demonstrations. In the beginning, it was just a mixture of different ex-college athletes and some powerlifters, but it turned out to be an extraordinarily effective tool, particularly in reaching young men. We also had the early beginnings of what later would be called GX International, a mixture of dancers, skateboarders, and BMX bikers. All these teams were still concepts that hadn't yet been fully developed, but they were fully operational in my pioneering mind.

We were truly living our lives with a Hebrews 11:1 framework: "Now faith is confidence in what we hope for and assurance about **what we do not see**" (emphasis added). There was a sense in our hearts God was going to make all of this happen, but in the natural it almost seemed impossible.

In time, our simple efforts began to pay off. The city of Spooner agreed to a springtime campaign in their local high school. It would be a three-day event with a different YWAM team each night, and I would preach and give the altar call. The local churches formed committees, the budget was raised, and we began a regional ad campaign. We even printed free tickets and put them in grocery bags in the stores. By the time the three-day weekend arrived, the town was buzzing about what was coming.

The first night was a Friday, and the large gymnasium was filled to overflowing with kids. The strength team performed a dynamic show and gave their personal testimonies. I preached the message, and when I gave the altar call, almost four hundred young people pressed to the front. Many were weeping as they surrendered their lives to Christ. The second night saw an even larger crowd. The dancers managed to pull off a show, I preached, and once again the altar was packed with kids repenting and turning to Jesus.

Sunday's program was Island Breeze. This time, it wasn't just kids but full families in attendance. Just before I went backstage, I took a quick trip to the men's room. While I was in there, I noticed something strange. There was a young man wearing a trench coat, even though it was seventy degrees outside. When I looked closer, I saw a rifle tucked under his coat. I quickly ran out and grabbed one of the volunteer police officers who was working the event. They came, questioned the young man, and arrested him. They discovered he had planned to shoot somebody on stage that afternoon. The show went on as planned. Island Breeze was dynamic, and several team members shared their testimony. I preached, and hundreds came forward, including two young men who had been a part of the shooting plot. They prayed to accept Jesus, and then the police quietly placed the boys under arrest. I was grateful the Lord exposed this demonic assignment before somebody got hurt. The teams were shocked when they later found out what almost happened, but we all concentrated on the wondrous things the Lord had just done. In a little town of just three thousand, hundreds of young people would never be the same.

After Spooner, we had testimonies from pastors and videos of the actual campaign, all of which gave credibility to what we were doing. Soon, cities all over the Midwest were opening up. By this time, I had recruited young workers to be my coordinators for these city campaigns. They came from Northern Europe, Australia, and various parts of North America. Even in the YWAM world, word was getting out that something big was happening.

We rented an empty nursing home building near our base to serve as dorms for the dozens of students who were coming for DTS. These schools multiplied our staff rapidly. With new staff, quality promotional material, and a lot of excitement, we aggressively went after new cities. The first ten cities came on board, and then twenty more. At each of the main campaigns we booked satellite events in little towns around the main hub. Now, our three teams combined could do ten or twelve outreaches a week. Thousands were coming to Christ. I had never seen anything quite like this in all my years of working in the United States.

The evangelistic teams quickly came together in a more professional way, growing their team members, working on choreography, and producing media. Our coordinating staff learned marketing, and we were doing major ad buys around each of the campaigns. By 1997, we were doing more than eighty cities a year just in the United States, with over seventy thousand recorded decisions for Christ. We were also expanding into six countries in Europe, plus Australia, India, and parts of South America.

We started a program to train campaign coordinators, another to train evangelists, and another for media and production. We had a video truck with full production capabilities parked outside our main campaign sites. The size of our auditoriums were growing in some cities. We were filling venues of five thousand, seven thousand, and even 10,000 for multiple nights. In the two-thousand-seat high schools, we often had to do two programs in one night just to serve the crowds that were coming.

One of the best parts was that Loren Cunningham would sometimes come to our large campaign locations and do an afternoon call to international missions. I produced an professional-looking video that went alongside Loren's teaching. It was called *Global Link*. We were not only helping to reach the next generation, but we were also exposing them to global missions and calling them to help reach the world with the gospel.

By this time, it had become clear to all of our leadership that being based in a remote location in northern Wisconsin wasn't conducive to domestic or global outreach. Soon, God would send a buyer to purchase our campus on behalf of a Christian ministry that worked with youth. What we had built was developed perfectly for what they had in mind. The businessman who purchased our base became a very good friend who later helped me build a major campus in Brazil and continues to play a key role in other parts of the world for YWAM.

The question at hand was, where should we go next? It seemed that God was leading us to get closer to the international aspects of YWAM, which led us to the largest base, located in Kona, Hawaii. This move would connect us with the islands in the Pacific and many other countries. It would prove to be vital in the next thing God would call us to.

God was now leading us on an extraordinary journey that would seemingly continue for the rest of our lives. He had taken our simple steps of faith and multiplied them into one of the largest evangelistic movements in the world. Little did I know, it was just the beginning.

Chapter 7

Radical Faith

I had just returned home from one of my many international trips and was sitting down to dinner when the phone rang. On the other end of the line was Jim Stier, international chairman of YWAM at that time, calling from Brazil. He got straight to the point: "Mark, why don't you bring the Impact World Tour to Fortaleza, Brazil?"

"When?" I asked. "Impact World Tour would be perfect for Brazil!" I had only started IWT a few years earlier. The Lord had given me strategic understanding of how to deliver the gospel in a relevant way to the younger generation using the arts, entertainment, and sports. Our "preachers" were not dressed in suits and ties; rather, they were skateboarders, dancers and strong men.

"May of next year," Jim answered matter-of-factly.

Immediately, my mind went into overdrive thinking of the already overwhelming schedule of IWT campaigns in front of us. It usually took three to five years to find and train the necessary staff and build the infrastructure for a major citywide campaign. We were already understaffed, stretched thin across more than seventy different cities on three continents. The idea of adding one more nation in the next year, especially one the size of Brazil, seemed absurd. It just didn't make any sense. I'm a risk taker by nature, willing to go out on the limb to try what others say is impossible. But even I was hesitant and wary about taking such a leap of faith. "Jim," I answered, "I would love to pioneer IWT in Brazil. But that sounds a little soon. It can take us several years to get ready for a campaign. How big is Fortaleza anyway?"

"Two, two and a half million," he responded.

"Two million! That's a big city. That would be a huge campaign, requiring an equally huge budget." I quickly answered. Already I was building a case for *not* bringing IWT to Fortaleza. No one in their right mind would consider taking on such a large project with such a short timeline.

"A lot of the work has already been done by one of our missionaries," Jim quickly assured me. "His name is Tony, and he's a YWAM base leader in the city. He's raising a budget of a million dollars. The churches are already on board with him. Would you at least pray about it?"

Knowing *that* was a question I couldn't refuse, I agreed, "Uh, yeah, sure, I'll pray about it." I respected Jim and his leadership in Brazil, and he had proven himself to be an apostolic pioneer in the nation. Because of his leadership, thousands of Brazilians had gone out into the nations, including some of the hardest and darkest regions of the world. Jim was a tough, no-nonsense missionary. I didn't want to dismiss his request so quickly, but my human reasoning had already taken over. I kept my thoughts to myself, but I simply couldn't see it happening.

After saying our goodbyes, I sat in the chair in my bedroom and had a one-way conversation with God. I explained to Him all the reasons we should not go to Fortaleza. "Lord, You know we don't have the staff or any coordinators who speak Portuguese. Besides that, it takes two years to set up a city of that size and raise that kind of budget." Even while I was telling God these things, I had a sense in my heart that I was missing something.

A Change of Mind

October, November, and December went by. Jim didn't call back, and I wasn't about to call him. I had already convinced myself the idea of bringing IWT to Fortaleza was so impossible that it wasn't even worth serious consideration. When January rolled around, Karen and I did what we often do at the beginning of a new year: pray and ask the Lord to bring correction and any necessary alignment. I also asked Jason, one of our young coordinators, to join me during one of these prayer times. I told him about Jim's ridiculous suggestion, and he laughed with me.

Jason and I had been praying only about thirty minutes when we both grew very quiet. The presence of the Lord felt heavy and strong. "Jason, what are you getting from the Lord?" I asked.

He hesitated, then sheepishly answered, "I think we're missing God on this Brazil thing."

I had gotten the same message. The next hour was filled with repentance and surrender to the plan of God for the city of Fortaleza.

To Jason's credit, he decided that he and his wife could go to Brazil and lead the campaign coordination. "Karen would love Brazil!" Jason said. "Let me call her." After a few minutes of conversation and prayer, Karen was on board. The couple, along with their two children, would head to Brazil to help launch the Fortaleza campaign. They didn't know a word of Portuguese and needed to raise the funds for airline tickets and living expenses. It would be the first step of faith, with many more to come.

The Faith for the Vision

A few weeks later, Jason and I boarded a plane for Brazil. We wanted to meet with Tony, the local missionary, and assess the city to see where things stood. We had no idea what to expect. Important planning months had already been missed. Little did we know the drama and adventure of faith that lay ahead of us.

When we walked out of the airplane terminal, Tony's smiling face was waiting for us. For several years, Tony was in his late twenties and had been building and leading a YWAM base just outside the city of Fortaleza. "It's so good to see you," Tony said warmly while embracing Jason and me with kisses on both cheeks.

We spent a few minutes sharing pleasantries, talking about our families and the city of Fortaleza. But once we were in the car, I got straight to the point, not wanting to waste any more time. Anxiously, I asked Tony, "Tell us, how are things going?"

Tony paused. "It hasn't gone as well as I had hoped. We are a little short on the budget."

"What's 'a little short'?" I asked. "How much of the million-dollar budget have you raised?"

Tony looked down and replied, "Actually, none."

"None? What do you mean, 'none'?" I asked, my voice raised slightly.

"We had a plan, but it didn't work very well. We were going to sell T-shirts and videos, but they didn't sell like we thought they would," explained Tony. His happy disposition turned downcast.

"You must have sold some," I pressed. I was hoping there was some kind of silver lining to the story.

"We did, but the money went to pay for the office space," Tony said. I could hear the discouragement and embarrassment in his voice. I could also hear Jason groaning in the back seat of the car.

In the hours that followed, we learned the rest of the story. Fortaleza, Brazil, was scheduled to host a gathering of YWAM missionaries from all over the world, including the top leaders in the organization. When Tony heard the conference was coming, he began to dream about reaching the city, using these missionary leaders as speakers. After much prayer, he and his staff believed God was showing them that one hundred thousand people would come to Christ in Fortaleza the same year as the conference. Acting on this word, Tony began meeting with church leaders in the city and persuaded them that a great move of God was coming.

But as the months dragged on, any seeds of faith that had been planted in the hearts of those pastors began to die. Only nine of the original seventy were still involved, and even they were starting to doubt what Tony said he had received from the Lord.

As we settled into our hotel in downtown Fortaleza that first night, both Jason and I were filled with all kinds of emotions, ranging from anger to confusion. None of this made any sense at all. We had spent money to fly to Brazil and were now wondering if it had been for nothing. After complaining to each other about the situation, we thought it best to pray. The first ten minutes of our prayer time was filled with questions.

"Lord, what do you want?"

"Did you lead Tony?"

"What do you want us to do?"

Then God's presence began to fill the room. We could both sense God had a big plan for the city and for the nation of Brazil, and that we were somehow meant to be a part of it. As we prayed, our anger and confusion were replaced with an understanding of what God had shown Tony. God had indeed given Tony a vision and faith to reach the city—not because he knew how, but because he was willing to be used by the Lord.

At one point in our prayer time, I looked out the window of our hotel room. Ten stories below, I could see young boys and girls standing on the street corners. It was about eleven o'clock in the evening, and I thought to myself, *Why are such young kids out on the streets alone at night?* Then it dawned on me: these children and young teenagers were being sold as prostitutes. My heart broke. These ten- and eleven-year-olds were the same age as my own kids at home. God reminded me that what we were doing wasn't about putting on a big event, but was really about reaching children like these. I shifted away from my pragmatic thinking and allowed myself to feel the Father's heart for these kids. Now I knew we had to reach Fortaleza. This campaign had become personal.

At the end of our prayer time, Jason and I knelt down and recommitted ourselves to the challenging task ahead. That night, we took a leap of faith into the unknown. We had very few answers, but we were excited. Sleep came easily that night; we both knew we were in the will of God. "Now faith is confidence in what we hope for and assurance about what we do not see" (Hebrews 11:1).

Preparing for the Campaign

I woke up early the next morning, eager to make the most of the rest of our time. My doubt and confusion were gone. Now it was time for full-on military mode. The next several days were filled with pastors' meetings, strategy sessions, and physical preparations. We helped Tony redo his plans and bring the pastors back on board. Jason and other staff members from the United States and Europe began making preparations to move to Brazil immediately. We had to become a spiritual army.

When international staff and their families arrived, they hit the ground running, beginning four straight months of fifteen-hour workdays. Reaching the city would take lots of time, discipline, and hard work. But more importantly, it would take a miracle. God had to lead us in battle and supernaturally open up the doors to the city. We also needed a financial breakthrough.

Prayer 24/7

We set up 24/7 prayer in the IWT downtown office where Christians from the city could come seven days a week to pray. Eventually, more than four thousand people were part of our around-the-clock prayer chain, asking God for an outpouring of His Spirit in Fortaleza. The movement of prayer coming alongside the missions strategy for the city was the key. "My house will be called a house of prayer for all nations" (Isaiah 56:7).

Soon, there was an electric atmosphere of faith. Nearly two hundred churches from all over the city got involved, working and praying together. The army of God was rising up. In all, almost ten thousand volunteers stepped forward to work in eleven different communities around Fortaleza. Jason oversaw 152 church fundraisers across the city in just fifteen weeks. Unpaid bills Tony had accumulated were getting paid off, and the necessary campaign funds were coming in.

City Saturation of the Gospel

The main evangelistic event would be held in the center of the city, in the forty-thousand-seat football arena. The Generation X, Team Xtreme, and Island Breeze teams preached at the local schools and prisons. The members of these teams represented four continents. This cross-cultural mix, along with the citywide television advertising, made them celebrities. School kids followed them and hung on their every word. More than twenty-five thousand school kids surrendered their lives to Jesus in three weeks. One school superintendent even called the campaign office to ask if he was too old to pray the prayer of surrender to Christ.

Island Breeze, who use their cultural dance and presentation to preach the gospel, was invited by some local government officials to perform at the cultural center for the city staff. Many gave their lives to Christ. Team Xtreme, who use sports and feats of strength to present the gospel, performed for 1,500 military police. The team leader, Keven Stark, preached powerfully, and more than two hundred soldiers responded, including the general. He walked up to the microphone and gave his own altar call: "I know what it means to be under authority. I have come forward to surrender myself to the supreme authority of all, and I believe many more of you need to do the same. It's time to stand up and come." After the general spoke, four hundred more military police stood up and walked forward.

Ministry was taking place all over the city—in the schools, government centers, military installations, and marketplaces. Thousands were coming to Christ before the main event even got started. The move of God that Tony had seen in his prayer time months earlier was coming to pass.

The Main Event

Friday night was the beginning of the three-day stadium campaign in the city center. Several hours before the program was to begin, the youth of the city lined up in the streets, waiting to get in. The traffic was near gridlock with so many people coming into the city for the event. When the doors finally opened, it only took twenty minutes for the entire forty-thousand-seat stadium to be filled. When I arrived an hour before the program, the doors to the stadium were already closed.

"Mark, what are we going to do? The stadium is full, and people are still arriving," one of my coordinators told me.

In the moment I decided we would need a second show that night. I told the IWT coordinators, "They'll have to come to the second show at 8:30 pm. Get the ushers together and tell them to go outside the arena and let people know."

That first night, about sixty thousand people heard the gospel. During the altar call, each of our three thousand counselors were working with two or three people at a time. In the three weeks of outreach, over thirty-eight thousand people came to Christ. The international Christian leaders who were in town to attend the YWAM conference were moved by what they were seeing.

True transformation had come to the city. Many of the youth who had just met Jesus were already sharing their faith at home, school, and work. The number of people coming to Christ continued to grow, even after the campaign. The seed of the Word of God was multiplying rapidly. Those trained as counselors continued to witness. Tony's dream, given to him by God, was coming to pass. Only eternity knows how many came to Christ that year, but many believe it was likely more than one hundred thousand—just as God had revealed to Tony.

The Move of God in Brazil Continues

The impact of the Fortaleza campaign could be felt across the region. Three hundred and fifty miles down the Atlantic coast from Fortaleza, Christian leaders in João Pessoa heard what had happened and desired the same for their city. This beach community of 800,000 was filled with young people. It was the perfect place to go next.

After what we witnessed in Fortaleza, we would need grounds big enough to hold the massive crowds. We were able to secure a large field which could comfortably hold twenty thousand people. Little did we know what God was about to do. The news of the awakening in Fortaleza was spreading. Prayer meetings were packed out and filled with enthusiasm. Committees were filled quickly, getting everything ready. Preparation was almost effortless. It seemed like the Holy Spirit was the wind at our back.

Our teams had just returned to the US mainland to recover after the very taxing two-month blitz of Fortaleza, but they turned around and came back to Brazil for João Pessoa. As before, they visited the local schools in the daytime, doing shows, presenting of the gospel, and giving altar calls. The response was overwhelming: thousands of kids came to Christ. The news media was everywhere covering the awakening, interviewing young people who had been rocked by the presence of God. Once again, our work in João Pessoa was on the evening news, in the newspapers, and on the radio.

It was becoming clear that the field wouldn't hold the crowds that would surely be coming. We scrambled and brought together the committee leaders and pastors, and decided that we should do two programs a night, back-to-back. As we had predicted, people were lined up, waiting to get in, on opening night. The field was packed for both programs. The altar calls were so large, we hardly had space for the people who came down.

I was busy running in every direction, overseeing a myriad activities. Not only was I administrating, I was also the stage MC, giving instructions for the altar calls. There was so much activity on the stage with all the teams coming and going that I had given strict instructions to my staff not to let anyone else on stage, particularly members of the media. Almost as if we were rock stars, everyone wanted access to our teams for interviews. Up to this point, the media had treated us well, but I knew from past experience that things could change in a moment if someone decided to do a hit piece on us. We experienced that very thing in Europe, parts of Asia, and North America.

On the second night, while giving instructions from the stage to the hundreds that had come forward, one of the local committee members walked onto the stage and tapped me on the shoulder. "Someone wants to interview you," he told me.

"They can wait," I responded, "I'm busy with the altar call."

"They're from *60 Minutes*, and they're behind you on stage." I looked at him with disbelief, because I had given instructions not to let anyone from the press on stage. *How could this happen?*

I turned over the altar call responsibilities to someone else and began to walk backstage. My mind was racing... *60 Minutes? One of the most watched television broadcasts in all of Brazil? They're known for doing negative reports on Christian leaders.* I was starting to get angry, so I had to regain my composure before talking to the program anchor. On the side of the stage, there were multiple cameras set up for an interview.

I could see the *60 Minutes* newsman sitting in his chair, waiting for me to sit in another positioned about four feet away. He was in his fifties and had a stark, handsome appearance. He had long, wavy hair with just a touch of gray, and his shirt was unbuttoned halfway down his chest, exposing the gold chains he wore around his neck. While I was walking toward him, someone from my team pulled me aside to let me know this guy was a very famous television personality in Brazil. I walked up to him and said, *"Olá!"* practicing some of the little Portuguese I knew. I settled down into my interview chair with a translator next to me. The news anchor began with a series of pointed questions, "What is Impact World, and who are these teams? Why did you come to Brazil?"

I had done hundreds of media interviews over the years, so I began to give my very rehearsed response. "Our teams are volunteer athletes who come from different countries around the world. They give their time on these tours to help young people. They share messages about a drug-free life. They're all Christians, so they come with a biblical perspective."

Interrupting me, the anchor said, "I know what they do, and I know what they preach. I was here for the full program. You're doing evangelism, and they're confronting areas of sin in peoples' lives." I could tell by his tone that he didn't like what our team members were saying. It seemed to me he had an anti-Christian, secular perspective on what was happening. I decided at that moment I might as well go for it.

I looked at him and said, "You're right! They do talk about Jesus, sin, and repentance. They talk about the living God and what it means to have a relationship with Him. They call young people away from their empty lives of sexual immorality, drug use, and partying. We not only call them to repent, but we pray for them and lay hands on them when we can." As I continued talking, I looked up at his face and could see that he was beginning to cry. Suddenly, he started to say something in Portuguese and all the cameras turned to focus on him. Now, he was openly weeping while he spoke. I pulled the translator near me and said, "Tell me what he's saying."

"He's telling the audience that he was a Christian as a younger man, but he walked away. Now, he's coming back and surrendering his life to this Jesus you were talking about." I was stunned. In front of me was this hard, worldly reporter, surrendering to Jesus for millions to see.

He continued, "Not only am I giving my life to Jesus, but you should too!" He then said to me, "Tell them what they should do!"

All the cameras turned and flipped on me, so I preached, telling them about Jesus and how they could exchange their life for a new one that He would give them. Then, I looked at the camera and said, "I'm going to pray with you right now. Wherever you are, watching this program, pray with me." For several minutes, I led them in prayer through my translator. When I finished, I said, "Amen."

Then, to my surprise, the interviewer said to me, "Now pray for them for the fullness of the Holy Spirit that you talked about." With excitement, I introduced the viewing audience to the Holy Spirit and prayed for them. Once again, the interviewer jumped in and said to me, "Now pray for those who are physically sick, that God would heal them." I paused for a moment, surprised that all of this was actually happening on a *60 Minutes* television broadcast, but I jumped right in and did exactly what he said. I prayed for the viewing audience that God would meet them and heal them right where they were.

The host closed out the broadcast and came over to me. He gave me a big hug and thanked me for what I was doing. After he left the stage with his crew, the local committee members came up to me excited about what the Lord had just done. We were all amazed at the move of the Spirit happening here in Brazil—and deeply grateful He would allow us to be part of it. Later that night, we all went to a restaurant on the beach and ate pizza. We thanked God while some of the younger members on our team danced and celebrated.

Some weeks later, I found out that this *60 Minutes* broadcast was aired unedited. It was so popular that the public asked if it could be aired again. It was aired twice more. Not only had tens of thousands been impacted through the campaign, millions more had the opportunity to hear the clear gospel on *60 Minutes*. God had taken our small, seemingly foolish efforts and impacted many across Brazil.

Chapter 8

Whole Nations

Rolling, green hills dotted with grazing sheep, crystal clear water lapping sandy beaches, and majestic mountain peaks of South Island make New Zealand one of the most pristine and beautiful nations on earth. No one who's been there wonders why famous movies like *The Lord of the Rings* trilogy, *The Hobbit* movies, and *The Chronicles of Narnia* entries were all filmed in New Zealand. There is no place like it. Besides being known for its natural beauty, it is also the adventurer's capital of the world. Extreme sports enthusiasts come to enjoy bungee jumping over steep canyons, rafting over dangerous river rapids, ziplining through forests, and heli-skiing off mountains. There is always an adventure to be found in New Zealand.

New Zealand is also one of the most remote places on earth and necessitates flying many hours through multiple time zones. I took my first trip to the country in February of 2000. I had been invited to a leadership training school in Auckland. Loren and Darlene Cunningham, the founders of YWAM, were there as special guests. It was on this trip that Loren asked me a question that would change my life.

Loren Cunningham

One day during the school, Loren spotted me and invited me to have lunch with him. I consider Loren to be one of the greatest missionary statesmen of our time. I also consider him a spiritual father and count him as a friend and comrade. We love to dream together about nations. In our conversations, there are no limits to what God can do.

He drove me to the local Denny's restaurant, his favorite lunch spot. We found a table with more privacy, where we could talk uninterrupted. My conversations with Loren were never short, so I expected to be there for a while. Right after we ordered our meal, Loren began reciting the history of New Zealand. "Did you know that at one time New Zealand sent out more missionaries per capita than any other nation in the world?" he asked. He then told me about the moral and spiritual decline the country had gone through over the last decade. Loren was a great storyteller, but he never just told a story for the entertainment value; he always had a significant reason for telling the stories he told. At this point, I'd known Loren long enough to know there was a reason he was telling me the story of New Zealand. Finally it came.

"Mark," Loren said with tears in his eyes. "What you're doing with Impact World Tour could really help this country. Would you consider working to re-evangelize New Zealand?"

I knew what he was asking. He wasn't suggesting I do a few local outreaches over a couple of weeks. My apostolic mentor and friend was asking me to reach a whole nation for Jesus.

Loren was aware of how IWT had impacted several other nations. From our first campaign in the state of Wisconsin, we moved across the United States and then to places like Australia, Europe, parts of South America, and Asia. Using entertainment, sports, and the arts, IWT brings what every heart desperately needs: Jesus. Young people fill schools, outdoor venues, and stadiums all over the world to see our teams perform; many of them leave knowing the Savior.

Whole Nation Strategy

Loren's question was a big one, and its answer would have a lot of ramifications. I knew that he was very serious and was asking for something that hadn't been done since the heyday of Billy Graham's ministry. Reaching a whole nation would take a supernatural move of God. In the natural realm, it would take millions of dollars and a large army of experienced staff to coordinate the effort. I had done enough comprehensive evangelistic campaigns in my life to know some of what this would take, but I had never tried to reach a whole nation.

If I said yes, I would be taking on a project without any existing financial or human resources. We had no current staff in New Zealand, no office space, and no local relationships to help us pull off such a feat. But I had learned never to make a decision based on the amount of money in the bank or the number of staff at the ready. I needed to hear from the Lord.

At YWAM, hearing the voice of God is one of our highest values. We believe that God still speaks today in a variety of ways. It could be impressions in the mind, dreams, visions, or a word from another person, but when God speaks, it's always in agreement with Scripture. He never contradicts Himself.

I looked at Loren and gave him the answer he expected. "I will pray about it," I told him. God would have to speak and verify this assignment was actually from him. I couldn't be flippant about something so large and life-altering for myself and those around me. Loren, Karen, some local Kiwis (slang for New Zealanders), and I spent that night and the next morning praying. By that time, we felt the Lord had made it clear this was from Him.

In May 2000, we launched Impact World Tour: New Zealand—without any money, resources, or staff. Thankfully Ross, a young YWAM staffer who already had experience coordinating campaigns in the United States, volunteered to come to New Zealand to help me launch IWT. We started meeting with church leaders and, to my dismay, no one we talked with believed New Zealand could be re-evangelized. The church in New Zealand seemed to be on life support, with little or no faith to be found. The spiritual condition of the nation was weaker than I had anticipated.

Just as I was coming to grips with the apparent lack of faith in churches across the country, I received a phone call from Ross. "Mark, do you have a minute to talk? I have something important to tell you."

"Hi Ross," I answered. "Sure, how have the meetings with the pastors been going?

Ross got really quiet. There was a long pause, and I could sense there was about to be another nail in the coffin. "Well, My dad offered me a place back working with him on the farm. Because of things happening with my family and personal life, I need to take him up on it," he said.

My heart sank. I felt my faith slowly deflate as Ross gave me the details behind his decision to leave. Now I really was alone. I told Ross I understood and wished him the best. I hung up the phone and sat there for a while, stunned. *Did I miss God? What should I do now?*

I spent the months of June and July praying for wisdom and breakthrough but received no clear answers. I didn't want to force something to happen, yet I still felt this mission was God's heart for New Zealand. I was fighting discouragement and started questioning the timing of the Lord, even His will. I did what many believers do when things reach an impasse. I prayed, "Lord, would you give me a confirmation about re-evangelizing New Zealand?" Satisfied that I did the best I could, I then set New Zealand on the back burner in my mind and went off on my next international trip.

I flew to the Netherlands in late July to take part in Billy Graham's Amsterdam 2000 gathering with ten thousand other leaders from around the world. Staying at our YWAM Amsterdam De Poort base allowed me to mingle with other international YWAM leaders who had come for the event. During the evenings, when the conference was done for the day, we would go back and fellowship in one of the many meeting rooms at the YWAM base.

One night, I stayed up later than usual. Next to me was Dave Cole, a Kiwi and senior leader in YWAM, now based in Singapore. Relaxing after dinner, we broke into a conversation about what each one of us was doing. After a few minutes I asked Dave, "Is it true you were once part of planting and leading YWAM bases in New Zealand?"

"That's right, Mark. We worked for many years pioneering YWAM on both the North and South Islands."

I began to feel a prophetic stirring in my spirit, sensing that, somehow, this conversation was ordained by God. I asked Dave,

"Are you aware of the project Loren has asked me to take on? He wants me to bring Impact World Tour across the country of New Zealand to help re-evangelize the nation." Dave sat up in his seat and suddenly became very interested. We spent most of the next hour talking about what God might want to do in his home country. I found out later that Dave and his wife Sue are very sensitive to the Lord. Sue, in particular, has a very strong prophetic gift. If they feel something is from the Lord, their answer is always yes.

Dave and Sue, like my wife Karen and I, have six children. So saying yes to any calling, especially one involving a change of location, is more complicated. I felt the need to be more direct with Dave. I looked him in the eye and said, "I would like you and Sue to pray about returning to New Zealand and leading this nationwide project."

Dave responded, "Don't you already have leaders in place?"

I told him that the project was so new we hadn't had time to develop staff. I made it clear that this was a pioneer effort: "We have some international IWT campaign coordinators who are willing to move for a season to New Zealand, but what we lack is a national director familiar with the country. A mature and seasoned leader is needed, someone who would have favor in the nation. Most of our workers are young and not from New Zealand. Dave, maybe you could be the director for the New Zealand Impact World Tour."

Dave seemed a little stunned but told me, "I'll have to pray about it with Sue before I can give you an answer."

What I was asking Dave had no natural or worldly appeal. YWAM missionaries traditionally do not take a salary, but instead raise their own support. Dave had been in YWAM many years and knew very clearly that there was no financial reward or incentive to saying yes. I was asking him to do something difficult: to move his family of eight back to New Zealand and receive no financial reward for their sacrifice.

Before the end of year, God had dramatically confirmed with both Dave and Sue that they should move back and lead this effort. God knew we had to have leadership who would stay in faith and never quit, no matter what the circumstances. Dave and Sue Cole are just such people.

Preparation Begins

In early 2001, Dave and Sue packed up their family and moved from Singapore to Auckland, New Zealand. Their first responsibility after getting settled was to find a building for the national office and begin running crash courses for new coordinators. Each trained coordinator would then be sent to live and work in a designated city or region.

Jenny Mollison, an Australian, was one of our seasoned campaign coordinators. With her amiable personality and commendable work ethic, Jenny was the perfect choice to serve under Dave. She was the only one on this new staff who really knew what it would take to pull off a nationwide effort of this magnitude. Through his relationships in the country, Dave found an office requiring a monthly rent payment of exactly zero dollars. It was located in an old industrial area of Auckland. The drab, gray, four-story building became the IWT national office for the next two years.

The small staff and new coordinators-in-training jumped in to help clean and paint. Local Christian volunteers helped too. Auckland churches donated tables, desks, telephones, computers, and other equipment. It was a humble beginning, but the Lord was providing for our needs.

Everyone knew God would have to open up the country supernaturally. During the three years of preparation, there were two forty-day nationwide fasts. Most of the Christians in New Zealand didn't participate, but enough did to shake things loose in the country. All of us knew that without significant intercession, this nationwide initiative would never happen.

Racial Reconciliation

One of the devil's strongholds in New Zealand was the racial division between the native people of the land, the Maori, and the Westerners who came largely from Europe. Just as it is in many other countries of the world, healing was needed. God made it clear that we should seek an invitation from the indigenous Maori leaders from across the county. This would not only give us favor with the native people, but invoke a greater blessing.

John Dawson, a native New Zealander and a senior leader in YWAM, was key in this reconciliation process. Using biblical principles, He knew how to go through "the spiritual gates" of the nation. John was the founder and director of the International Reconciliation Coalition. He had written several books on racial and ethnic reconciliation. He and a local Maori elder traveled throughout New Zealand on what they called "the Maori Gates Tour." They went to Maori communities across the country to honor the people, ask for forgiveness, and request favor to "come into the land." This took humility and time, but the effort brought a measure of healing and unity to the church in New Zealand. We started to see the wall of division crumble. Protocols included a speech by a local elder, formalizing their welcome, ceremonial pressing of noses for the exchange of the breath of life, and sometimes a feather is placed in front of the guest who then picks it up to indicate the receiving of the welcome. Often all of this is followed by a long meal cooked over heated rocks in a deep pit. Great favor was released over Impact World Tour as the elders in the Maori communities officially welcomed us into the land.

An Army Called to Action

With significant intercession going on and new favor from the native people, cities across the country began to inquire about IWT. Our newly trained coordinators had to carry numerous cities on their own, many times with demands far beyond their natural capacity. I began to make personal phone calls to some of my other staff in North America, Europe, and South America, asking if they could come and give a year and a half of their lives. Many of them responded to the call and said yes. With no time to waste, they packed up their families and quickly moved to one of the IWT cities across New Zealand. It was a small but faith-filled army, determined to see God move. Each of us felt we were part of a historic move in the nation, but we took 1 Corinthians 1:27 to heart: "But God chose the foolish things of the world to shame the wise; God chose the weak things of the world to shame the strong."

The next big hurdle was finance. To cover the entire country over a twelve-week period, it would cost over three million US dollars. We knew this had to be raised locally, city by city, but the New Zealand pastors were already struggling to meet their own budgets. Their congregations had been dwindling, leaving them with their own intimidating financial challenges.

We really needed some kind of financial breakthrough from God. Finally, it came at a fundraiser at the north end of South Island. A small group of a hundred and fifty people committed to give more than eighty thousand dollars to evangelize their region. For New Zealand at the time this was a miraculous outpouring. This news quickly spread all across the country. No one believed this kind of money could be raised in New Zealand. The Lord was answering our prayers. People heard about the eighty thousand, and it sparked faith that the same thing could happen in their communities too. Within just a few months, our young staff operated like a military unit heading out with their assignments. The young army dispersed all across the country, speaking at fundraisers of all kinds. The financial needs were beginning to be met.

Often on my trips to New Zealand, I would crisscross the country, speaking at fundraisers almost daily. Frequently, our bookkeeper, Brian, would call Dave and me to tell us how much money we had to have by the end of week, and sometimes even by the end of the day. Time after time, a check would arrive in the mail or someone would stop by the office with the exact amount we needed. We were on a true journey of faith. We believed God is faithful, and we were seeing His faithfulness in action.

As a team, we believed every bill must be paid, and we did our best to pay them on time. The twelve-week tour began in the last week of January 2004. By then, we had only been able to raise one-third of the national budget.

Dave Cole had a reputation for having high financial and moral integrity—and he also had a reputation for being optimistic and filled with faith. He always stayed steady, and I never once heard from his mouth any words of unbelief. Impact World Tour in New Zealand had the right director to carry it through. He was a true warrior.

Hard Work and Faith

By the grace of God, our fifty ragtag, mostly young, and inexperienced staff had to organize the whole country for an evangelistic campaign. Together, they had:

- Completed more than five hundred church presentations
- Mobilized almost twenty thousand volunteers
- Prepared 1,500 church-based discipleship programs
- Trained more than ten thousand counselors
- Made arrangements to house five hundred team members in fifty-three different cities
- Prepared stages, performance ramps, sound and light rigs, and a transport fleet

In addition to fundraising the national budget, each of our workers had to raise their own support. There were no hired professionals of any kind on our staff. Every aspect of this campaign had to be built by faith, not by sight. "For we live by faith, not by sight" (2 Corinthians 5:7).

By tour time, fifty-three communities across New Zealand were hosting city-wide events with more than 110 booked stadiums and auditoriums. Our two sound teams traveled in large semi-trucks with massive staging and public address equipment. Our large evangelistic teams had their own vans, trailers, and trucks. This was a major operation.

Over the course of twelve weeks, the three evangelistic teams of Island Breeze, Team Xtreme, and Global Xpression International would be doing hundreds of outreaches in schools, prisons, and stadiums across the nation. In all, there were more than 470 people on tour, including DTS outreach teams that had come from around the world.

The Holy Spirit Comes

Finally, it was January 18, 2004, the day we had all been waiting for: the Impact World Tour launch event. Early that morning, I walked out into the courtyard of the Auckland YWAM base, ready to address our various teams. I was met by a Maori warrior in full dress. He was there to welcome me officially on behalf of the tribe. It was then that the unseen wind of the Holy Spirit came, and suddenly my legs began to shake. I dropped to the ground on my hands and knees.

The presence of the Lord was so intense that I just couldn't stand up. Looking around, I noticed no one else seemed to be having this experience. I crawled on all fours, pulled myself up onto a chair, and beckoned the worship leader to come over and talk to me. I told her that the Holy Spirit was moving, and she needed to start singing. I am sure I looked ridiculous. She seemed puzzled, but she could see me shaking and immediately went to the microphone. I don't remember what she sang—some familiar worship song—but within minutes, the intense presence of the Lord moved over the whole crowd. The singing, crying, and spiritual groaning of the crowd became so loud, it could be heard blocks away from the courtyard. It was like a war cry being released from the young army over the nation.

Loren Cunningham and John Dawson, who were staying in a nearby guest house several blocks up the hill, heard the noise and came down to see what was going on. When they walked into the courtyard, they were caught up in the same presence of the Holy Spirit. This spontaneous move of God went on for four hours.

That evening, there was a public meeting for Christians in Auckland to welcome Loren Cunningham and the other international guests.

A large auditorium was packed to overflowing. As the meeting began, the same move of the Holy Spirit we had experienced that morning in the courtyard erupted once again and went on for several hours.

We were marked by God. All of us knew this tour was not going to be like any other we had ever experienced. Something powerful was just beginning, and we were all caught up in the middle of it.

After the Auckland meetings, the whole IWT army of five hundred moved to the first campaign city, Gisborne. This city, on the eastern edge of New Zealand, is known as the place where the sun rises first each day. It is a significant city to the native Maori people and was important to them that IWT begin here.

The manifest presence of the Lord we had felt in Auckland stayed with us into Gisborne. Our preparation meetings were powerful, with dynamic worship and a tangible presence of the Lord. We felt we were riding on the wave of the Holy Spirit.

24/7 Prayer

Several days before the campaign began, I had another unexpected encounter with the Lord. I was woken out of a deep sleep by an inner audible voice. It was the Lord speaking to my heart. He told me that I was to call Mike Bickle. Mike is the founder of the International House of Prayer (IHOP) in Kansas City, Missouri, which hosts prayer rooms and prayer meetings twenty-four hours a day, seven days a week. I felt I should ask Mike to have the prayer warriors at IHOP lift up the New Zealand tour 24/7 for the duration of the campaign.

I knew that Mike did not like to interrupt the normal flow of the prayer room. The mandate of 24/7 prayer required discipline, structure, and routine to keep it going. If he was going to say yes to my request, I knew it would be because God had spoken to him.

I asked YWAM international leader John Dawson, a close friend of Mike's, to join me on the call. Before the end of the week, the three of us were on the phone, connecting from multiple continents. John Dawson was the first to speak. He had a limited amount of time to be on the call, so he got straight to the point: "Mike, I know you know Mark, but I want to tell you the role he plays in YWAM. The evangelistic ministry he began is called Impact World Tour. It's the tip of the arrow leading YWAM into new initiatives, and Mark is the tip of the tip."

Immediately Mike jumped in. "John, would you say that again?" John repeated himself, and after a brief pause, Mike continued, "I can't believe it. For three months, our leadership team here at IHOP has been getting prophetic words that we should connect with 'the tip of the arrow.' We have been searching the Scriptures, trying to figure out what that meant. Whatever your request is, the answer is yes!"

A moment later, John had to say goodbye to both of us and hung up. I spent the next ten minutes telling Mike the story of preparation for the New Zealand campaign and then shared with Mike what the Lord had told me several days earlier. Mike responded, "Wow! Twelve weeks—that is a long time! I would need our leadership team to agree on this one. Can you come and present this to them this Sunday night?"

He had no idea what he was asking me. Meeting with his team meant flying back to the United States and then immediately returning to New Zealand. Normally it could take up to seventeen hours to get to New Zealand from Kansas City. Round trip, my already jet lagged body would rack up thirty-four hours of flying. But this was too important. I knew. no matter the cost, I had to say yes. "Okay, Mike. Where is the meeting, and what time should I be there?"

One day later, I flew home to Kansas City. It was an all-night trip, so I arrived seriously jet lagged and went straight to the IHOP elders' meeting. To my delight, Mike had already spoken with the leadership team, and they were excited and already committed to praying for the tour for the next twelve weeks. They told me God had brought them to Zechariah 3–4, and that the prayer movement was like Joshua standing before the Lord as high priest. They said I was like Zerubbabel, holding a plumb line in my hand. When the people saw the plumb line they would rejoice (see Zechariah 4:10)! I was so tired, I didn't get it all, but the Lord would confirm that specific word out of the book of Zechariah two more times in the upcoming weeks.

We agreed in the meeting that I would give the IHOP team daily prayer requests and praise reports from the field. This partnership between missions and prayer would prove to be one of the most important aspects of the whole campaign. It felt like we were aligned with heaven, doing things the way God had always intended. The enormous battle that we were beginning had to be won in the spirit realm in prayer and intercession, and then on the ground with faith and hard work. Little did I know how much warfare lay ahead.

Proclamation Begins

The first outreach in Gisborne began on a Thursday night, outdoors with a large crowd from all over the region. There was light rain during the entire program that only paused briefly during the altar call. More than twenty percent of the people in attendance came forward at the end to surrender their lives to Christ. Everyone was encouraged and excited about the coming days and weeks. The rain continued, and the sound crew quickly covered everything with tarps. Little did we know that the rain would follow us for all twelve weeks of Impact World Tour.

The next morning, we were all checking the weather reports, eager to know if the rain would continue. New Zealand has a reputation for having one of the rainiest climates in the world, and the weather forecast showed us why: a front was moving in and was supposed to stall out. It was possible it would rain for days.

Though it did continue to rain, the weather didn't keep the crowds away. Kiwis are known for being a hardy people. They're used to going about their lives, rain or shine. They came out in record numbers, and many came to Christ. Large groups from the Maori people came forward during the altar calls, responding to Christ. We could see how important it had been to go through the spiritual gates by honoring the indigenous people of the land. We gave a Bible to each convert and pointed them to one of the many local follow-up programs that were just beginning. Counselors contacted the new believers, overwhelmed with the number of people responding at the altar calls.

The teams continued to move throughout the country. We now had two separate traveling caravans to cover the many cities across New Zealand. Our goal was to reach every person in the nation. This seemed impossible, but we believed somehow with the Lord it could happen.

It Kept Raining

The rain continued in the cities of Marton, Opunake, Hawera, Wanganui, Patea, Dannevirke, and Hastings. The tour was now two weeks old, and the response to the gospel was more than anyone expected, but it still continued to rain. It seemed like it was raining harder every day. We kept praying the rain would stop, but then we started to wonder if the rain was sent as a sign from God.

Back at IHOP, the prayer room was packed and buzzing. There was growing excitement over what was happening in New Zealand as they heard the reports of hundreds and thousands filling the altars. The daily prayer requests and reports kept the prayer room humming. I made sure to ask them to pray for the weather.

The weather broadcasts were now reporting the storms across New Zealand were getting worse. Record rainfall was expected across the country. To understand how daunting these reports seemed, you have to know that out of the 110 venues we had booked, 98 were outdoors!

Should We Quit?

The tour now moved toward the capital city of Wellington on the southern tip of the north island. The city is known for its unpredictable and often nasty weather. Just north of Wellington, the teams performed outdoors in Hutt City. The crowds were massive, but the weather got even worse.

After the final night in Hutt City, the sound and light teams stored some of the gear and went to their guest homes to rest. During the night, an intense thunderstorm and record rainfall came through the event grounds. The winds destroyed the staging, and the field was turned into a mud hole with standing water everywhere. The trucks couldn't get in to remove the staging and skate ramps, the sound towers were bent like a pretzel, and water had gotten into the speaker boxes.

The campaign coordinators began receiving emergency calls from everyone. The tech crews were saying they couldn't continue the tour. Some of the young dance teams wanted to quit and go home. Pastors on the executive committees of the upcoming tour cities wanted to cancel their events. It seemed like chaos broke out everywhere, all at once. At the same time the weather reports continued to be discouraging. The meteorologists started to declare these storms as the worst rain the country had experienced in a hundred years. There were reports of record flooding everywhere. *Why weren't our prayers being answered?*

I got alone with the Lord and began to cry out. "What should we do?" I asked Him. I was prompted in my spirit to go to Deuteronomy 28:7, which says, "The Lord will grant that the enemies who rise up against you will be defeated before you. They will come at you from one direction but flee from you in seven."

I knew what we had to do. Instead of canceling events, we had to increase the number sevenfold! I called my lead coordinators and told them to bring together the executive committees in the Wellington area.

We met the next morning. I shared with them what the Lord had told me and challenged them that we needed to find indoor facilities in the area to use in the coming days. Kiwis are known for being fighters and warriors. They have a noble history of triumph in battle, despite often being outnumbered. They all began to rise up in new faith, declaring out loud that the enemy would not have the victory!

They immediately went to work with our coordinating staff, booking high schools, civic centers, anything suitable for hosting an event. It was starting to look like an emergency military operation. The body of Christ in New Zealand was going to war.

As predicted, the rain got worse. It poured hour after hour, but we would not quit, and the tour did not stop. These smaller auditoriums were packed to overflowing. Instead of defeat, all of the obstacles seemed to stir a greater hunger and boldness. Instead of shrinking back, we resolved to advance forward. The young people were hungry for the gospel, the presence of God was strong, and our evangelistic teams found new energy. "From the days of John the Baptist until now the kingdom of heaven has suffered violence, *and the violent take it by force*" (Matthew 11:12).

The Capital City

J. C. Ryle once wrote "The harvest of the Lord's field is seldom ripened by sunshine only. It must go through its days of winds, rain and storm." Heading into the capital city, we were still in the middle of our stormy days. Our big event was to be held in the most famous cricket and football stadium in the country, the Wellington Oval.

The day before the event, our teams tried to set up the 4x8 portable staging on the cricket grounds, but the weather had only gotten worse making it impossible to do the normal setup. Each time we tried, the sections would start blowing away. The wind was blowing, with gusts between 100 and 160 kilometers per hour. Instead of our usual staging, we had to move in a flatbed truck to use as a stage which wouldn't blow away. This was solid and much heavier, able to stand the windgusts.

Team Xtreme—a group of athletes and strong men who use feats of strength to present the gospel—was on the schedule for the first night. They were particularly effective in reaching young men, and their main evangelist for this tour was a large, young

Maori man named Jason. He was thrilled to see so many of his people coming to Christ across New Zealand.

Several hours before the opening night event was to begin, I went over to the stadium. I found a seat in the broadcast booth, where I could view the field clearly. The weather had now turned into a serious storm. The rain slammed against the booth window, and the howling winds caused the glass to move back and forth. It was clear it would be impossible for Team Xtreme to do their normal performance outside on the cricket grounds.

By this point, I was spiritually and physically exhausted, as were the coordinators and the team members. Besides the many challenges of the on-the-road tour, which were almost unprecedented, we still needed more than two million dollars to cover our costs. The financial burden was always on my mind. I sat back in my chair and with a weak voice said to the Lord, "What should I do?" At that moment, as if an answer to prayer, my phone rang. I picked it up and said, "Hello?"

It was John Dawson. Without any greeting or introduction, he began declaring out loud to the unseen forces, "Satan, you are a liar. You will not have the victory. You were defeated at the cross two thousand years ago…" Prophetic intercession and declarations continued for almost fifteen minutes straight. After addressing principalities and powers in prayer, John said to me, "Mark, be encouraged. The victory is the Lord's!"

We then talked about what we should do with the event set to begin in just a few hours. We decided to continue on and preach to whoever came. Logistically, this would be nearly impossible, but we both knew we couldn't quit.

Warriors Arise

After the phone call, I walked down to the men's locker room to let Team Xtreme know we would have to change our approach that night and couldn't do the usual show. As I opened the locker room door, I could hear the members of Team Xtreme praying intensely for that evening's event. Some of the men were lying face down with their arms spread above their heads on the concrete locker room floor, slamming their fists while declaring God's Word.

I paused for a minute and just watched the strong men of Team Xtreme. In that moment, I knew something great was going to happen that night. The powers of hell would not be able to stop this nationwide evangelistic thrust! I was watching a spiritual violence rise up in that locker room; this young army was not going to quit.

That night in the Wellington Oval, the weather was everything they predicted. The wind blew, the rain poured, but to our great surprise nearly two thousand people showed up. They huddled under the overhang in the upper bleachers, though that didn't really stop the rain, since the wind blew it in sideways. Our sound crew rigged up some speakers under tarps in the front row of the upper deck, and the Team Xtreme members stood next to the speakers to preach. There was no performance—that was impossible without a stage and in the bad weather.

Jason grabbed the microphone. He stood six foot four and weighed more than three hundred pounds. His Team Xtreme muscle shirt was completely drenched in the rain, his long, jet black hair whipped around in the wind, and water poured down his face as he spoke. He gazed fiercely through the howling wind and rain. The warrior spirit of the Maori rose up within him, and he fearlessly declared the gospel. Then, he looked up suddenly, pointed at the weather, and said, "Rain, stop!" Within a few seconds, the rain stopped falling. There was a pause in the weather. He turned his eyes to the people in the bleachers once again and called them to come forward.

People got up and walked down through the puddles. They came by the hundreds and stood in the rows at the bottom of the bleachers. Jason led them all in a prayer of surrender to Jesus. Counselors then came out from the weather-protected walkways with follow-up materials and decision cards, and prayed with those who made decisions for Christ. Not one person who came forward was dry, but they didn't seem to care. There was a warrior preaching, and now there were new warriors responding to the gospel. These people were serious. The harder the message and the more difficult the environment around them became, it seemed the more they wanted to respond. After the final person had filled out their decision card, it was like the invisible pause button was lifted, and the rain began to pour again.

I met with Team Xtreme, the coordinators, and some members of the local executive team in the locker room after the program. We all knew this was a turning point in the whole campaign. From that day on, everyone had new determination. "But we do not belong to those who shrink back and are destroyed, but to those who have faith and are saved" (Hebrews 10:39).

Rain and Harvest

In the weeks that followed, the number of tour towns increased. Through the month of February every outdoor event had rain, but the New Zealanders didn't seem to care. Word about a move of God had traveled through the country, and the people in these little cities didn't want to miss it!

When we got to the city of Tauranga, Loren Cunningham was sitting in the front row with a group of business people. This was a great encouragement to everyone who had been laboring so hard for the past several weeks. We felt we had finally turned a corner. From that time on, it felt like the wind of the Holy Spirit was at our backs. We saw victory after victory. By this time, thousands of Maoris had come to Christ. We were being told this was the first time in the Maoris had responded like this to an evangelistic campaign. Another great victory was that God sovereignly met all of our financial needs before the campaign was done. It was now clear this would be the largest evangelistic thrust the nation's history.

It was now evident that entire countries could be contended for. New Zealand is a small country, but this campaign showed us that with God all things are possible. His leading and divine strategy, along with our faith and determination, brought victory in battle. One of the greatest lessons we learned is that there is a price to pay, but the victory is the Lord's if we don't quit!

The prayer warriors at the International House of Prayer prayed 24/7 for twelve weeks, just as they promised. They didn't quit either. This, no doubt, was the biggest key to our finishing strong. As far as I'm concerned, the missions movement and the prayer movement can no longer be separated; the two movements must become one for the sake of the gospel's advance. It was a lesson I learned back then and am still learning today. It's lesson I will never forget: in order to contend for the nations, missions and prayer must come together. "My house will be called a house of prayer for all nations" (Isaiah 56:7).

Chapter 9

God's Design: Prayer and Missions Together

New Zealand is a relatively small nation, so news of Impact World Tour (IWT) spread quickly from city to city. Local news stations and national newspapers were reporting the phenomenon. Headlines read: "High impact extravaganza"; "Crowds thrilled by high-flying stuntmen"; "Enthusiastic response to IWT"; "Shows deliver action, message about choice"; and "Xtreme message after extremes in weather."

We began making final preparations for an event in the city of Tauranga. This beautiful city, with its wide, sandy beaches, rests on the east coast of the North Island. By the time Karen and I arrived, the place was already teeming with IWT staff and team members, busy meeting with executive leadership teams, setting up sound systems, organizing fundraisers, and following up with the thousands who had already responded to Christ.

One morning, while Karen and I were having our early morning prayer time, the Lord impressed it on our hearts to go on a one-day fast. We were still in the middle of an intense campaign schedule, and my phone was ringing constantly. There were still substantial budget needs to be met, and there was always some kind of problem to be fixed. It would be hard to unplug from the frantic pace, but we both knew it was the right thing to do.

I called the leadership team together and explained that Karen and I would need to take the next day for prayer and solitude. The local coordinator found us a small condo a block away from the beach where we could get alone, be quiet, pray, and listen.

The next morning, we walked into the one-room condo and began to worship. I had been going on adrenaline, so it took me a while to quiet my mind and focus on the Lord. As I paced back and forth in the living room, asking the Lord for wisdom, suddenly I heard a sentence in my spirit: "My house will be called a house of prayer for all nations, or it will not be My house." I immediately recognized the first part as taken from Isaiah 56:7, but the second part was new.

While I was still trying to sort out what it could mean, the Lord impressed the message on my heart again. I now knew it was important and the reason the Lord had called us into this time of fasting and prayer. I turned toward Karen to tell her what had just happened. She was across the room, face down on the carpet and apparently shaking. This was not her normal posture in prayer, so I sat next to her and waited; I could tell something very deep was happening.

About five minutes later she sat up, still shaky and teary-eyed. "What happened?" I asked.

"God spoke to me. It was so clear. It wasn't audible, but His words were so clear in my mind."

Now she had my full attention. "What did He say?" I inquired.

"My house will be called a house of prayer for all nations, or it will not be My house," she said.

I was shocked. "Karen, you won't believe what God just said to me. He spoke the exact same thing!"

Now we really felt like we were on holy ground. It wasn't just excitement at hearing God's voice; we had a greater sense of the fear of the Lord. But still, we wondered what the phrase "or it will not be My house" meant. Was it a rebuke or a warning to us? Did God want to warn the church as a whole that it must be a house of prayer for all nations or it wouldn't be His house? The message had more of a correcting and warning tone than an encouraging or comforting one. It left us shook up with questions swirling around in our minds.

One thing we did know: this was a defining moment related to the convergence of missions and prayer. It wasn't merely about the importance of having intercessory prayer meetings for missionaries or countries around the world; it was about the very essence of what God's house is. My mind flooded with understanding. The global church was to be a house of prayer for all nations. God was not only telling us what His church was meant to be, but He was also putting special emphasis on how serious He was about all this right now. Would He really stop considering the church His house if the church didn't take seriously His original design?

We spent the rest of the day praying over what this all meant. Now our prayer time was turning into a Bible study. *What do you do when God speaks?* The first thing we did was search the Word for confirmation and greater insight. We started with Isaiah 56 and looked at what Jesus said about the temple being a house of prayer in the New Testament. Then we went to the early church in the book of Acts to gain more understanding. We reviewed the Great Commission in Matthew 28:18–20 and considered "the great multitude that no one could count, from every nation, tribe, people and language, standing before the throne" in Revelation 7:9. Clearly, God's people being a house of prayer for all nations was a recurring theme in Scripture. It had a twofold meaning:

1. Whatever we called God's "house" has to have room for all people groups. People from every tribe, nation, and tongue will surround Him at His throne (Revelation 7:9). No one will be left out of His house.
2. God's church and Christian gatherings have to be focused on interceding for all the people groups of the world. Praying for the nations would open up doors of opportunity to the unreached.

Having worked with the organized church in much of the world, I knew this was the opposite of the way most people functioned. Church gatherings are some of the most segregated meetings in the world, and there is almost no intercession for lost people, let alone unreached people groups from the difficult and dark places of the earth. Most prayer is for personal needs or prosperity, not for what was on the heart of Jesus. "For the Son of Man came to seek and to save the lost" (Luke 19:10).

The church is largely ignorant of the various unreached people groups in the world. This lack of awareness, burden, and intercession is the main reason it has taken so long to see the Great Commission advanced around the world. If this biblical mandate could be restored, it would bring new life, growth, and purpose to the church!

The Young Army

In the weeks that followed this encounter, God began to give me more insight into this revelation. It became clear from the Scriptures and from watching our young missionaries preach the gospel that God was preparing a new generation of warriors. This would be a company of people who intimately know their God and do great things for Him! "The people who know their God shall be strong, and carry out great exploits" (Daniel 11:32 NKJV).

I began to call this next generation of believers "the young army." They would be a different kind of army. They were "warring worshippers," thirsting for real intimacy with God and burdened for the unreached of the world. This would be a group that rediscovered the dynamics of the New Testament church. The young army would be a fearless force that would preach publicly and work in signs and wonders. They would be unstoppable.

This understanding caused me to look back at how God had been leading me and my family over the years. I now understood why He prompted our move from Kona, Hawaii, to Kansas City, Missouri, in 1998, the year before the International House of Prayer began. God knew what was coming and wanted to show how the prayer and missions movement could function as one under His leadership without becoming the same organization. One new movement would be born in order to help the next generation of believers to rediscover God's original intent for His church: to become a house of prayer for all nations.

Chapter 10

What Would It Take to Finish the Great Commission?

Sometimes something as simple as saying yes to an invitation can change your life. That's the way it happened one morning when I walked into the office in March of 2000. Barb Livingston, the office administrator, greeted me. "Mark, you have a list of messages," she said. "One of them is from Billy Graham's office."

"Really?" I replied. "I wonder why they are calling?" I sat at my desk with the message in hand and began to dial the number of the Billy Graham Evangelistic Association (BGEA) in Minneapolis, Minnesota. While I was dialing, my mind flashed back to the year 1973, when I attended the Billy Graham Crusade at the Minnesota State Fairgrounds in the city of St. Paul. That day as a teenager, I walked forward with a group of my friends and made a public commitment to Christ.

"Hello, BGEA," the receptionist answered. A minute later, I was speaking with one of the organizers for a major event Billy

Graham was conducting in Amsterdam later in the year, called Amsterdam 2000. The goal was to bring together ten thousand evangelists from all over the world for a strategic conference in this western European city.

"Mr. Anderson, you have been recommended to be part of a special forum during the conference that Mr. Graham is putting together with six hundred international Christian leaders. These leaders will represent many nations of the world to discuss one important question: 'What would it take to complete the Great Commission?'"

I immediately had a stirring in my spirit and thought, *What a great question!* It was a question that I had been asking myself most of my ministry life. "I would love to!" I answered without hesitation.

"Great," he replied. "In the coming weeks, you will be receiving a series of questions. We would like you to respond before we come together in Amsterdam. At the conference itself, you'll be part of round table discussions with the other leaders from around the world." Just as he promised, a short time later I received a whole series of questions about the Great Commission. I carefully answered each one and sent them in, as did the hundreds of other leaders from around the world.

Amsterdam 2000

When I arrived in Amsterdam on July 29, 2000 and went to the venue for registration, I discovered BGEA had already processed my information. I was struck by the extraordinary efficiency. Later, I found out that my good friend Paul Eshleman, a leader for Campus Crusade for Christ (CCC), had organized the round table discussions. God had used him for nearly a quarter of a century to lead the *Jesus Film* and other video projects all over the world.

With ten thousand evangelists all in one place, the conference was buzzing with excitement. Western suits and ties and colorful African dress stood side by side. The atmosphere was alive with the nations, tribes, and tongues as we met each day in workshops and plenary sessions. It was an exhilarating experience.

In a side room at the arena, six hundred of us gathered around tables to answer the question, What would it take to complete the Great Commission? Each numbered table had about eight people and a table moderator, who led each of the discussions. Someone would present a key discussion point, and then we would work on solutions around our tables.

The information we had sent in advance had been compiled and was available to us in printed form during our discussion times. I love strategy, planning, and solving problems. The whole process was exciting and deeply engaging.

Table 71

Steve Douglass was the moderator at our table, which was numbered seventy-one. He had just become president of Campus Crusade International, following the death of founder and legendary Dr. Bill Bright. Steve and I had met before but never had the time to get to know each other. We quickly bonded as we bantered back and forth on these Great Commission issues. I discovered that Steve, like me, was very pragmatic and action-oriented. We would often be moving ahead with solutions while others were still discussing the question. Steve and I have become good friends over the years, and we still enjoy this same dynamic today.

It was on the third day of the roundtable discussions that something life-altering happened. All six hundred Christian leaders were given a list of the known untargeted, unreached people groups (UUPG's) from around the world. These UUPG's had no known Christians among them, no Christian-witness, and no Bible available in their language. These are whole groups of people who had not been reached in two thousand years of Christian history. They had never been engaged with the gospel, and no one was even targeting them.

Bruce Wilkinson, who at the time was the president of Walk Thru the Bible and had written the bestselling book "The Prayer of Jabez," and Paul Eshleman hosted the session. Paul began, "There are 232 known people groups in the world who have never had a chance to encounter Christ. They have had no evangelism and there is no church among them. This isn't right. In fact, they are not even being targeted even after two thousand years. This is direct disobedience to the Great Commission Jesus gave us."

After Paul finished bringing deep conviction to each one of us, Bruce Wilkinson took the microphone and challenged us, saying. "We in this room lead the vast majority of the earth's Christian army. What if each of us decided to adopt one or more of these groups? We have to make sure that each one of these groups is targeted before we leave this room today."

We were all asked to look at the list of people groups and pray about which ones to adopt. Then we were to respond by writing down the group name and handing it to Paul Eshleman, who was standing at the front. Over the next fifteen minutes, we all turned to prayer around our tables. I could see that some people representing mission organizations had begun to write. One by one, they began to make their way up to Paul to hand him their commitments. Volunteers sitting toward the front were busily adding up the commitment totals. Every few minutes they would hand Paul an updated number.

"We have our first three adoptions!"

"We now have twenty-eight adoptions!"

"Sixty!"

Each time a number was announced all the leaders started clapping and cheering. The room was electric with faith. Leaders were so excited that some skipped bringing their slips of paper to the front, and just stood and shouted out their commitments. One Christian businessman stood up and declared he would take ten people groups, which brought a loud "Amen" and more applause to the room.

It seemed to everyone victory was close at hand and soon the announcement would be made that all 232 untargeted, unreached people groups had been adopted.

Then, unexpectedly, the commitments stopped coming. No matter how much Bruce exhorted the leaders from the front, no one moved. Paul explained to us which groups were left to be adopted. It was clear these were the most difficult, in places where missionaries might go in but never come out. It was no mystery to anyone in the room why these groups were left.

There was an eerie quiet in the room. Some were praying, but most were looking around to see if anyone would take these final groups. Where at first there was almost euphoria and a sense of victory in the air, now felt like discouragement and defeat. I was sitting there praying that someone in the room would have the courage to say yes to these remaining people groups. While I was praying for someone else to take these remaining groups, I felt a tap on my arm. Steve Douglass, who was sitting right next to me, leaned over and said, "What if our two organizations took the rest?"

This caught me off guard. I was already extraordinarily busy at YWAM, working in hundreds of cities around the world. I was convinced I couldn't do anything more. The thought of working with remote people groups seemed impossible. How would I even process something like this in YWAM? We didn't have centralized, top-down leadership, like most of the missions agencies in the room that day. No one, not even our founder Loren Cunningham, could speak for the whole mission. Not only were we were decentralized in operation, but YWAM was by far the most diverse and international missions agency in the world. Even as the argument was still raging in my mind, I heard the still small voice of the Lord in my Spirit saying, "This is Me." I took a deep breath, turned to Steve, and said, "Okay, let's do it."

As I said the words, I comforted myself with the fact that this was a private conversation and I would have plenty of time to work it out with the international leaders in YWAM over the months to come. But unbeknownst to me, a moment later Steve Douglass signaled one of his Campus Crusade staff to take a written note to the stage saying Campus Crusade and YWAM would adopt the rest!

Paul stood up quickly and announced the exciting news to all six hundred leaders. There was a thunderous noise of joy that filled the room. I sat quietly in my chair, stunned. What I thought was a private conversation was now the talk of the whole conference.

Unity in the Church

Shortly after the announcement was made, we were given a thirty-minute coffee break. Steve and I used this time to discuss the Herculean commitment we had just made. I turned to Steve and asked, "If we're going to reach these groups, what does that mean? What will it look like to truly 'reach' them? What are the elements we need?"

"Well," Steve replied, "we would need new churches. The International Missions Board, the church planting arm of the Southern Baptist Convention that Avery Willis leads, would be perfect." At that very moment, Avery walked up to our table.

"Avery, we were just talking about you." Steve said. "We need a church planting movement in each of these unreached people groups." Without any hesitation, Avery replied, "I'm in." Avery immediately pulled up a chair and sat down to join our discussion at table seventy-one. Next, we all agreed we would need Bible translation. The obvious choice was Wycliffe Bible Translators, who handles the majority of Bible translation in the world. Just as we mentioned this, as if on cue, Roy Peterson, the president of Wycliffe, responded from a neighboring table.

"Roy," Steve asked, "can you help us with Bible translation for these unreached people groups?" Without even answering the question, Roy pulled a chair up to table seventy-one and began leading a discussion on how we could begin work on the Bible translations we'd need.

In the minutes that followed, others quickly joined our table. Bruce Wilkinson came over and volunteered Walk Thru the

Bible's resources. Steve Steele with Dawn ministries offered his organization's research on church planting. Several other ministry heads excitedly said they would help in any way they could. The Holy Spirit was moving.

We all realized we were part of an emerging miracle. In just a few hours, we had moved from zero focus on the untargeted, unreached people groups of the world to an alliance of major ministries committing together to complete this great task Jesus had given us two thousand years ago: "Therefore go and make disciples of all nations, baptizing them in the name of the Father and of the Son and of the Holy Spirit" (Matthew 28:19).

This was a great turning point and spiritual marker in my life and, more importantly, for the global church. I felt I was on a whole new adventure and knew my life in missions would be forever changed. Something supernatural was unleashed that day, something that is still advancing even now. The church came together and became a powerful army. "Since the time John the Baptist came until now, the kingdom of heaven has been going forward in strength, and people have been trying to take it by force" (Matthew 11:12 NCV).

Shortly after Amsterdam, Steve and I began to meet with a select group of leaders to continue planning our strategy. We called our group Table 71, the table where we sat on that important day in Amsterdam. It's now been over twenty years of meeting three times a year. We still meet to this day.

I was starting to see and experience the power of oneness—when the church comes together in unity as an army to accomplish what is closest to God's heart: the Great Commission. Our primary task was to find out how many unengaged, unreached (UUPG's) people groups there actually were in the world. We couldn't really lay out a strategy to help the body of Christ to engage each one until we knew what we were really dealing with. We discovered there were not just 232 UUPG's, but actually thousands across the world. There were more of these groups than we even thought. We also discovered several other things:

1. Very few people among these groups could read or write. Therefore, we had to adopt an oral strategy to evangelize and disciple them.
2. We found out there were many different lists of UUPGs. These had to be reconciled so we could work off one master list.
3. To reach these groups we had to enlist and facilitate nationals on the ground in each geographic region.
4. In almost every case, no portion of the Bible had been translated yet for these UUPGs.

We all worked diligently, with each member of Table 71 using their area of expertise to concentrate on solving these challenges. This took great humility. We had to lay down our own agendas—even our reputations—for the greater cause of the gospel. Later, I realized what we were really doing was laying down our merely human agendas for the higher agenda of God. I started to believe reaching those who had never heard the gospel was right in the center of God's heart and plan for the world.

Chapter 11

Seeing All

Have you ever been asked a question that changed your life? That happened to me in early January of 2007. I wasn't expecting anything to change or looking for something to be added to my life, but the Lord had other plans.

Dr. Bill Bright, founder of Campus Crusade (now Cru), launched the Global Pastors Network (GPN) in the early 2000s. Dr. Bright's dream was to bring together leaders from across the globe to work on finishing the Great Commission. I was asked to be on the board of the GPN along with other prominent leaders, including well-known leadership author and speaker John Maxwell and the new president of Cru, Steve Douglass.

GPN came out of the gate with a lot of energy, public fanfare, and events with prominent ministry speakers. But it soon became clear that GPN's vision lacked defined outcomes and strategies to implement the completion of the Great Commission. I am a strategic and results-driven person, so I was growing increasingly frustrated with the lack of clear action plans.

At one of the launch events, John Maxwell walked up to me and asked to buy me lunch. He said we had a lot to talk about. We made our way to a mostly empty restaurant in the hotel complex and found a table in the back corner. John began to bear his heart, "Mark, I'm the chairman of GPN, but I'm not sure what it is. I got involved because Dr. Bright asked me to, and now he's gone to be with the Lord. We need to get clarity on where this is going. Mark, will you help me redefine GPN?"

Everything John said was true. I had known it for some time, but out of respect for Dr. Bright, I had been hesitant to tell anyone. Over the next hour, John and I wrestled with what GPN could become if it were reorganized. One thing was clear: it couldn't continue the way it was going.

What John didn't know is that Karen and I were already praying about me stepping down from the board, and in the months that followed, we made that decision. I planned to call Steve Douglass, the president of CRU, in the first week of January 2007 and let him know. To my great surprise, Steve called me first.

"Mark," Steve asked, "Do you have a few minutes?"

"Sure," I replied, "What's going on?"

"Some changes are happening with GPN, and we were wondering if you would consider being the next president?"

I stuttered for a few moments, thinking back to a conversation I'd had with Karen just the week before about how excited we were for me to be stepping down from GPN. "Steve," I replied, "I'm not sure I can take on that responsibility." He was very gracious as we talked for another ten minutes, but he understood I was saying no.

One week later, Steve called again. "I know you declined the first offer, but we have been praying and still think you might be the right guy. Would you reconsider?"

"With all of the staff at Cru, surely you have someone who could take on this role," I said. "I'm part of YWAM, and this is a Bill Bright initiative."

"I would never want to hinder your work with YWAM," Steve responded. "Perhaps you could just add being the president of GPN to the rest of your responsibilities?"

As much as I respected Steve, I couldn't imagine adding more to my plate. Karen and other people who cared about me were telling me to take things off my plate, not add more things to it. "Steve, I'm sorry. I don't think I'm your guy."

After the phone call, I felt kind of odd and a little uncomfortable. *Am I missing something?* I thought to myself. *What is the Lord trying to say?*

To my surprise, Steve called again the following week—January 18, 2007, to be precise, a day I'll never forget. "Mark, I know you've said no twice, but would you please reconsider?" After a few minutes of conversation, I declined again and we said goodbye. What I was feeling now was more than uncomfortable; it was a clear sense that I was missing God, but I decided I could ignore it. I just needed to go home and rest. I called Karen and told her I was coming home to rest for the afternoon. She told me the kids had sports, so I'd have the house to myself.

I left the office, went home, had a little lunch, and sat down on the couch in the living room. I closed my eyes and, before long, I was sound asleep. Sometime later—I'm not sure how long—I was startled awake by a profound sense of God's presence in the room. I couldn't see anything, but I could feel it—a tangible, almost-terrifying conviction of God's holiness. Immediately, I hit my knees and began weeping. The only way I can describe it now is to tell you that the light of conviction was turned up so bright that I could see hundreds of areas of compromise and sin in my life. It was completely overwhelming. I collapsed. My face was pressed into the carpet, and I just wept and repented for two hours.

The entire time, the presence of God remained strong in the room. God was dealing with my thoughts, my motives, my sins of commission, and my sins of omission. By mid-afternoon, I wasn't even sure I was saved. I crawled on all fours into the den, pulled myself up into a chair and turned on some worship music. Sitting there with my eyes closed, I said, "God, I don't understand what's going on."

The Lord revealed to me the Great Commission calling He had given to Bill Bright and Loren Cunningham when they were young men. It's what drove them to become the men of God they had become. I understood what a privilege it was to be connected to YWAM and Cru, to interact regularly with Loren Cunningham and to have met with Bill Bright. All I could do was continue to repent.

I was completely overwhelmed and still trying to take in all that was happening, and then the Lord spoke to me in a voice that seemed to be audible: "The time has come for the Son of God to be revealed." I immediately thought of John 17:1, where Jesus prays, "Father, the hour has come. Glorify your Son, that your Son may glorify you." And then the prayer of Jesus in that chapter began to unfold in front of me, particularly John 17:21–22: "that all of them may be one, Father, just as You are in Me and I am in You. May they also be in Us so that the world may believe that You have sent Me. I have given them the glory that You gave Me, that they may be one as We are one." Suddenly the plan for completing the Great Commission became clearer to me than it ever had in my life. First, our goal must be to reveal the Son.

Second, we must become one with the Father and Son as they are one with each other.

As I sat there, the encounter continued. Before me was a picture, almost like a movie. I saw a great awakening of the earth, with tens of millions of people coming into the kingdom in a short amount of time. I saw endless youth, representing all the nations of the world. Their numbers were so vast that it was like looking at an ocean with no end in sight. This image shook me. By this time, I was shaking in my chair. Different emotions moved over me like waves. I was awestruck, filled with joy, and kept crying. I had never felt anything like this in my life.

With everything I was experiencing, I lost track of time. But then I noticed Karen had returned home and was standing at the entrance to the room. She had been there for almost an hour. She didn't see what I saw, but she was aware of God's presence and that something significant was happening. I looked up at her and tried to describe what had happened. "Karen, I think it has to do with the phone call this morning with Steve Douglass. God has an assignment for me. It must be related to taking the presidency of GPN."

She responded and said, "You must go to the people you really trust. You need to get confirmation from Loren Cunningham, John Dawson, and David Hamilton."

"I don't know how that's going to happen," I said. "Those are three of the busiest people I know. They're probably all traveling in different parts of the world."

"This is too important for us not to get that level of confirmation," Karen replied.

We were raising six kids and homeschooling, and Karen was feeling the burden of carrying the weight of that alongside my busy travel schedule. Taking this responsibility would bring more stress and perhaps other changes. It was crucial that we test this, so we both would really know it was God.

After a little more debate, I agreed, and we committed our plan to the Lord in prayer. The first one I called was David Hamilton, whom God has used to give global direction to YWAM. I remembered that he had a medical appointment in southern California, so I thought that, out of the three men, I would have the best chance of connecting with him.

David answered the phone right away: "Mark! How's the family?" After a few minutes of catching up on personal matters, I told him about my encounter. He immediately responded, "Well, that sounds like God to me."

"David, would it be okay if I flew out to California and met with you?"

He said, "Sure, I'm going to be here for several days while I finish some tests."

Two days later, I flew into LAX, picked up a rental car, and drove to where David was staying. After a couple hours of processing, I told him, "Now, I need to connect with John Dawson and Loren Cunningham."

"I think John is at home, here in Los Angeles," David told me. I called him immediately. To our great surprise, he answered the phone and invited us to come over, have a meal, and discuss the whole thing further.

The next day, Dave and I drove up to John and Julie Dawson's home. They were as warm and welcoming as always, excited to see us, and anxious to hear what God was doing. I was eager to hear John's prophetic insight into my situation and glean something from his many years of wisdom. After I shared my experience with the presence of the Lord, he exclaimed, "I think it's obvious you're supposed to take the role. It feels to me like God is going to give you a larger voice in the body of Christ across the world."

The next call was the hardest. Loren Cunningham could literally be in any nation on earth. After a brief prayer, I called his mobile number, and to my delight, he answered right away. "Mark! It's great to hear from you!"

"Loren, I know you're probably traveling, but I wonder if there's a way we can connect. Where are you now?"

"I'm in Vancouver," he responded.

"I'm in LA with John and David. Is there somewhere we could meet you?"

"Well, it just so happens that I'm going to be in LA in a couple of days," Loren responded. "Let's all get together Monday night. How does six o'clock sound?"

After confirming the time and place with John and David, I hung up the phone. We all sat there in John's house, amazed at the sovereignty of God to align all of our schedules in just a few short days.

We met on the top floor of a hotel in Pasadena, where we had a small meeting room all to ourselves. Loren was happy to see the three of us. After our short time of fellowship, Loren pulled up a chair across from me and said, "So, what's going on?"

I knew this conversation would be a bit different than my conversations with John and David. Loren Cunningham founded YWAM. It was his baby—and I was there asking for his input about leading an initiative started by another ministry. I decided to unpack the whole story of my encounter, including the conversation with Steve Douglass. The minute I finished, Loren jumped in and said, "This is God!" The four of us spent that evening dreaming and strategizing about what God might have in mind.

Flying home the next day, I had mixed feelings. I now had clear confirmation that I should take the presidency of the Global Pastors Network, but I wasn't excited about the opportunity. There was nothing appealing about the job offer—at least not in the natural. It would mean more work and responsibility, and as with all YWAM and Cru initiatives, there would be no financial reward. Both ministries are based on a self-funding model of income. In addition, I had spent the majority of my life working with pastors, but now I wanted to expand my influence by working with Christian leaders in others spheres, like business, education, technology, entertainment, and government. How could I do that with a network of pastors? What about the vision of millions of young people I had received? Everything in me longed to reach and disciple the next generation.

After arriving home, Karen and I committed all of these unanswered questions to the Lord, trusting that He would establish our steps. We didn't know it at the time, but we were about to enter the most fruitful season of our lives. We were not looking for a big change, but we couldn't deny that God was supernaturally ordering our steps. "In their hearts humans plan their course, but the LORD establishes their steps" (Proverbs 16:9).

Chapter 12

Engaging All

In December of the year 2000, I was asked to speak at the international gathering of YWAM leaders in Auckland, New Zealand, called the *Hue*, the native Maori term for "gathering." I was to follow Joy Dawson, a fiery intercessor with a strong prophetic gift. She was key in the founding and early development of YWAM. Her messages were always direct and often called for repentance. I knew whatever I was going to say had to be from the Lord, or it wouldn't flow following something from Joy.

In the days leading up to the Hue, God was dealing with me about the *all*'s in the Bible. For example, Matthew 22:37 tells us, "Love the Lord your God with *all* your heart and with *all* your soul and with *all* your mind" (emphasis added). Matthew 28:18–19 reads, "Then Jesus came to them and said, '*All* authority in heaven and on earth has been given to me. Therefore go and make disciples of *all* nations'" (emphasis added).

Jesus does not call us to reach *some*, but *all*. And He does not call us to give Him *some* of our heart, but all of it. Because these commands seem impossible on the surface, I had spent many hours in prayer and meditation seeking to understand, with the help of the Holy Spirit, how obedience to these commands could even happen. I knew Jesus would not give us commands just to frustrate us.

On the day I was to speak, it was as I expected: Joy Dawson had a direct and timely word from the Lord. She challenged everyone listening to repent of complacency and embrace anew the original vision of YWAM to go into the whole world. YWAM leaders from around the globe poured forward in the auditorium, kneeling, prostrating themselves, and even crying in repentance and recommitment to the call of global evangelism. Some stayed at the altar through the lunch break, allowing the presence of the Lord to penetrate deeper into their hearts.

After the break, we had a brief prayer time, and then I was introduced. I had felt the hand of the Lord on me all day, and the sense of God's presence grew even stronger as I listened to Joy's message. What she said set me up perfectly to be bold about what I believed God was saying, "As a global movement, YWAM was not called to reach *some*, but rather to lead in reaching *all*— and to do it with completely surrendered hearts." If we were serious about this, we had to map out the Great Commission, measure our progress, and go where no one has gone before.

Loren Cunningham, YWAM's cofounder, and David Hamilton, a key leader and one of the great strategists in our mission, were sitting in the front row. As I was speaking, the Lord was giving concepts and ideas to David, and he typed them out on his laptop. Loren was moving forward in his chair, poised to jump in and give a shout of "Amen!" to what I was saying. At the end of my challenge, I felt prompted to invite Loren up on stage. He not only gave an *amen*, but he added history and context for the YWAM global family.

In the weeks that followed, David Hamilton mapped out the Great Commission in a measurable way, using four thousand geopolitical zones. These became a roadmap not only for YWAM, but later for the larger body of Christ.

After my January 18, 2007 encounter with the Lord and the confirmations from David, John, and Loren, I called Steve Douglass and took the role of president of the Global Pastors Network (GPN). As I stepped into the role, I knew the many partners of GPN, which represented hundreds of significant Christian leaders, were all wondering, *What's next?*

It was weeks later, in May of 2007, that the next step became clear to me. I was meeting with David Hamilton about the next steps for GPN and how they related to YWAM and its global call. David had his laptop open and said, "Mark, have you seen my friend's new logo? He has a real gift in this area." While he was talking, he turned the laptop around for me to see. Across the top it said, "call2all," pushed together as one word.

Immediately, I sensed the Holy Spirit telling me this was it—a call to all of the body of Christ to reach all of the world! "David! Would he give me that logo and branding for a global movement?" I asked. "We need to gather Christian leaders from across the body of Christ to work together to complete the Great Commission. We need to do this across the world and in every region."

David and I moved into strategic planning for what would become the call2all movement. "Let's roll GPN into this as a pastors' network, but let's also do networks in the other spheres of society like business, education, government, family, and media," I said. In 1975, both Loren Cunningham and Bill Bright had received a word from the Lord about reaching the seven spheres of society. God had separately called both men to take a time of prayer and fasting in Colorado during the same week to give them a deeper understanding of the Great Commission mandate to disciple all nations. This revelation was foundational in the development of Youth With A Mission and Campus Crusade for Christ.

David and I began to brainstorm what would later become Document 777, a holistic definition of the Great Commission built around the spheres.

Seven themes that Jesus gave us

1. Prayer
2. Evangelism
3. Bible Engagement
4. Growing Christian Community
5. Compassion and Justice
6. People Groups
7. Unity and Humility

Seven spheres of society

1. Family
2. Education
3. Economics (business, science, and technology)
4. Government
5. Celebration (arts, entertainment, sports)
6. Media
7. Religion

Seven geographic all's

1. Countries
2. Zones
3. Districts
4. Communities
5. Neighborhoods

6. Homes
7. Individuals

These three "sevens" overlapped, bringing a clear, measurable framework for the Great Commission. In the days that followed, I began a new nonprofit around call2all. I began talking to many key leaders in the body of Christ, particularly those heading up missions movements, about the idea of convening leaders in "congresses."

One of the key people was Paul Eshleman, executive vice president of Campus Crusade for Christ and founder of the famous *Jesus Film* Project, which has been viewed more than seven billion times and translated into more than 1,800 languages. His specific passion was to be sure that every people group in the world was engaged. "Paul, I think I have a way to mobilize the global body of Christ to adopt the unengaged, unreached people groups of the world."

"What's that?" he replied.

"Let's do a series of congresses—three-and-a-half-day gatherings—in every region of the world. We'll bring together top Christian leaders to educate them on the unfinished task of the Great Commission. We'll call them to action, and we won't stop until every people group is adopted, every Bible translation is completed, and every part of the world has a church planting movement."

David Hamilton and Paul Eshleman became key players in the call2all movement. We identified and mobilized many of the world's top Christian leaders to participate in the congresses and the ongoing Great Commission activity. These were mature leaders who had already proven themselves successful in their various callings but who were now willing to come together with one another on a much greater level to see the completion of the Great Commission.

Plans were laid for the first congress to be held in Orlando, Florida, in honor of Dr. Bill Bright, who had gone to be with the Lord. Northland Church was excited to host this first gathering. They had caught the vision of call2all and proved to be the perfect hosts for the first Congress. Key ministry leaders in the body of Christ such as Loren Cunningham, Luis Palau, Jack Hayford, and Steve Douglass, along with the heads of major agencies and denominations, participated. In all, we had more than six hundred key leaders with an astonishing 172 presidents and CEOs!

For three and a half days, these key leaders gathered around tables to pray and strategize global evangelism using the 777 framework. New relationships were formed, and the atmosphere was electric with fresh vision and faith. Amazingly there was no division, disunity, or competition of any kind. There was a true John 17 unity around the common objectives Jesus gave us. During these three days, I realized a movement was beginning, one that could help the body of Christ move to the next level of advancing the kingdom. Though mentally and physically exhausted from all the preparation, I was filled with gratefulness to the Lord for what He was doing.

Seven years earlier in Amsterdam, Steve Douglass and I, along with five others, committed not merely to talk about the Great Commission, but to do it. We were committed to action until all the finish lines were crossed. In that spirit, we took several hours on the last day of that first congress in Orlando and asked the six hundred delegates to pray at their tables about specific commitments they would make to see the unfinished task completed. At the end of prayer time, we gave them commitment forms to fill out that they were to bring forward during an altar call. Groups at each table contended in prayer until they had clarity about what God wanted them to do. Notable leaders humbled themselves before the Lord and made great leaps of faith, often beyond the resources they had in hand. Many were adopting people groups that had never been engaged in all of church history, some in very difficult areas of the world. A miracle was happening in front of our very own eyes. At the end of the three and a half days, leaders had committed to:

- Bring the gospel to 762 million people
- Plant 1,378,000 new churches
- Adopt 3,512 unengaged, unreached people groups
- Undertake 9,590 Bible translation and engagement projects

Those of us who had worked on this congress were elated and a little bit stunned at what had just happened. We had tried for years to bring people together like this, often with great frustration. Now the church was coming together and doing something they could only do, operating as one body.

As the commitments were being tallied and announced, we all began to praise the Lord and worship. Some even jumped up and down at what God was doing! People were grabbing their phones and cameras, taking pictures of the tallies that were up on the screen. There was new faith in the room that the Great Commission could really be accomplished.

Word of what happened in Orlando spread quickly to Christian leaders in America and around the world. More congresses happened in quick succession in East Africa, Canada, Brazil, and Ukraine. Similar miracles took place in each of these locations, and extraordinary commitments were made to bring the Great Commission across the finish line.

Preparation began for a large global congress to be held in Hong Kong in 2009. Asia, of course, has seventy percent of the world's population. China itself has 1.4 billion people. We decided we needed to have room for 3,000 delegates, all of whom would sit at round tables. This would require an indoor facility three times the size of a football field. We also agreed there needed to be 120 workshops to cover the key subjects related to the fulfillment of the Great Commission.

As I boarded a plane in Kansas City to make the twenty-four-hour trip to Hong Kong, my mind raced with many thoughts. Would we find an auditorium big enough? How would we mobilize Christian leaders from more than a hundred countries? What about the underground church in China? Could those leaders come? Where would the massive budget come from to pull off an event of this magnitude? I said a brief prayer and committed all of it to the Lord, then laid back and closed my eyes to rest during the long flight ahead.

Our first organizational meeting was held in the Hong Kong YMCA. We had strong representation from the church world as well as the marketplace. These leaders had heard reports about what happened in Orlando and some of the other cities of the world and were hungry to see the same happen in Hong Kong. In typical Asian fashion, everyone who came was extremely organized and willing to do the hard work necessary to make an event this large happen.

The next day, I toured a massive new conference center in town. As I entered, I knew it was the place for the call2all Congress. The place was so large that we had to drive golf carts to get around.

It not only had an open auditorium for three thousand to sit at tables, but it had more than a hundred breakout rooms. The big question was: What was the price?

Accompanied by several high-end business leaders in Hong Kong, we spoke with the management of the conference center to see what kind of deal could be reached. Because the facility was brand new, they were willing to negotiate a rate well below the going price for the Hong Kong market. The rate was still was hundreds of thousands of dollars, and we had yet to price sound systems, lighting, buses, conference equipment, media, advertising, and twenty or so other major expenses, but it was a great start and gave us faith for all that lay ahead.

When I went back to my room at the YMCA, I reflected on all the Lord had done and was once again amazed at how He acts on our behalf when we say yes to His assignments. In just two short years, we had gone from the idea of gathering Christian leaders together to map out the completion of the Great Commission to seeing the dream come alive in many different regions of the world. Now we were on the verge of drawing together thousands in Asia. I had a clear picture of how the mustard seed of faith works. "Faith comes by hearing, and hearing by the Word of God" (Romans 10:17 NKJV). When faith comes, it has to be spoken and acted upon, which is planting the seed. Then, it grows quickly and becomes a tree for many to perch in.

After we secured the hotel and conference center, the hard work of mobilization began.

Who should we invite to make up the 3,000 delegates? The big nation—China—was right in Hong Kong's backyard. We had to have strong representation from the millions of Chinese believers, but the trouble was that most of them were living underground—

particularly church leaders. While there was some openness, there were still many being arrested for their faith. You could tell that any openness was only temporary and that the communist government would clamp down on the believers harder in the future, particularly as more tracking technology became available.

We decided to invite people from more than one hundred countries, including the Indian subcontinent, all throughout Indonesia, the Philippines, North and South Korea, Myanmar, Thailand; the list was exhaustive. We determined the number of invitations for each country based on the country's population.

The senior leader in YWAM in Asia was Tom Hallas, an eclectic Australian with a great sense of humor. I gave Tom a call, "Tom, did you hear about the call2all Congress we did in Orlando?"

"Yes, mate. That sounded exciting!"

"We're planning one in Hong Kong, but this time with three thousand people. Would you help me identify the key leaders across Asia?"

Tom supplied context for key YWAM leaders in many of the nations in the region. "Mate, you need to give Loren a call and tell him to send out an invitation to our lead YWAMers."

"That's a great idea, Tom! I'll do exactly that."

I flew to Kona, Hawaii, and made my way from the airport up to the Cunningham home. I was greeted by Darlene. "Mark! Welcome! Come on in, Loren is expecting you." Darlene showed her typical hospitality, offering me my favorite beverage and a snack. Loren was in the living room with a notepad at his side.

"Loren, our next Congress is going to be in Hong Kong. I'd like to ask you to be one of the presenters—and to send out invitations to the key YWAM leaders in the region."

"Of course!" Loren responded. He picked up his yellow pad and began to write down the names of leaders, country by country. It was amazing to watch him quickly jot down those names. Loren had personally visited every country on earth, and he retained an intimate understanding of every one. He also remembered the names of the main YWAM leaders. "There's Silo in Bangladesh. He should bring a group with him. He's actually Samoan, you know. There's Steve Goode in Thailand. He's American but has lived in Thailand for years and knows everybody. Steve and Liz Cochrane can help us in India." It was clear that Loren understood call2all and what God had called us to do. His apostolic anointing was fully engaged.

Loren grabbed his phone and started making calls. He had an expansive list of the personal phone numbers of YWAM leaders around the world. In just a few hours, we were able to get positive responses from key leaders all across Asia. Our mobilization was in full swing.

In the months that followed, I spent a lot of time in Hong Kong. I love the pace of that city. Our team was well trained and efficient, and we were able to connect with some very influential Christian businesspeople who opened doors most pastors could not open and helped us gain favor with hotels, transportation companies, and vendors for the auditorium. Prayer networks in Hong Kong and around the world were covering the Hong Kong congress with intercession. I called my good friend Mike Bickle, the founder of the International House of Prayer in Kansas City, and asked him to include Hong Kong in his regular prayer sets. He had been with us for the original launch in Orlando, so he was quite aware of what a congress looked like and what it could accomplish.

The day before the Congress was to begin, I spent some time sitting in the foyer of the Marriott hotel, watching the delegates check in. The enormity of this congress struck me suddenly. This was going to be one of the largest gatherings of its kind in church history! With people coming from more than a hundred different countries, we would have simultaneous translation in six different languages. I had just received word that the number of delegates from China was approaching eight hundred, most of whom had never left China before. I said a quick prayer: "Lord, may this congress be everything you want it to be."

Early the next morning, I went to the auditorium and noticed that the Chinese delegates were already arriving in buses from the neighboring hotel. I asked their team leader why they had come so early, and he told me they wanted to intercede in the auditorium each day for one hour before the Congress started. I was just beginning to understand how different the church in the East is from its counterpart in the largely complacent West. The Chinese church was almost extinct under Mao Tse-tung, and now there were about one hundred million Christians in the nation. These were a different breed of believers who daily risked their lives to follow Jesus.

By nine o'clock, the vast auditorium was packed with people at tables as far as I could see. On the floor in the middle of the auditorium was a massive vinyl map of the world. It was large enough for four thousand people to stand on. I was told it was the largest map of its kind ever printed. On the map were the countries, then the geopolitical zones, and finally the locations of unengaged, unreached people groups. Engaging with this map, those gathered would intercede for nations, receive callings from

God to adopt unreached areas, and have times of praise, prayer, and declaration. We gave each delegate Post-it Notes so they could write down what God said to them and stick it on the global map. By the end of the first morning, the large map was filled with hundreds of words of the Lord, many related to personal callings to the nations.

The congress's leadership team knew God was moving in a very supernatural way. One of the things that really struck us was the level of unity in the room. There were people from more than one hundred counties, and despite great ethnic diversity, language differences, and a variety of ages, everyone worked in unity to push toward the completion of the Great Commission. At the end of the first day of the three-and-a-half-day gathering, leaders were already adopting unengaged, unreached people groups in some of the hardest areas of the world. They were also thinking about pioneering new church planting movements, strategies for engaging the lost in Asia, and starting new houses of prayer. The afternoons were spent in workshops—more than a hundred of them—learning best practices for the key areas of the Great Commission. There were also breakouts of the newly formed business, media, and education networks.

The afternoon of the third day was spent in prayer, listening to the Lord, and making our faith commitments in the main areas of the Great Commission. What would we do within three years? Within ten? The time culminated with an altar call, where delegates brought their written commitments forward and handed them to senior leaders in the body of Christ. They made a covenant before the Lord that, with His help, they would accomplish all that He had placed on their heart to do. Every ten minutes, we would look at the tally on the screens, and the room would erupt in applause and praise. The final commitments were:

- 4,130 unengaged, unreached people groups would be engaged
- 1,643,000,000 would be reached with the gospel
- 434,000 new church churches would be planted
- 161,000 new prayer watches or houses of prayer would be started
- 99,000 new oral Bible teams would be sent out

Later that night, it hit me. We had just finished one of the largest international gatherings for Christian leaders in church history. Slumped in a chair in the green room of the Hong Kong Marriott International Convention Center, I thanked the Lord He helped us bring more than three thousand leaders from more than one hundred countries, including several closed nations.

I was sitting there, drifting away, and almost asleep when someone tapped me on the shoulder. It was a key leader from YWAM, reminding me that I had one more meeting with the YWAM staff who had come from across Asia. I shook myself awake and slowly walked over to the coffee pot to get one more cup—fuel to get me through the next hour. I was then led out to a waiting golf cart and driven to the meeting room where the global leaders of YWAM were waiting. I was a few minutes late, but as I entered the room, they all began to clap. Overwhelmed by this show of affection, I walked to the front, where John Dawson was moderating. He had me sit in a chair while Loren Cunningham and other senior leaders surrounded me and laid their hands on me. One after another, they shared words of encouragement and scriptures, and they prayed that God would prepare me for whatever lay ahead with this movement that was making its way across the world. It wasn't until that moment that I began to realize the magnitude of what God was doing, as well as the stress I was carrying. The spiritual warfare I'd been engaged in had taken its toll. It was clear that the battle for the nations, to advance the kingdom of God, was real and required just as much bravery and sacrifice as a tangible world war.

Lying in my hotel room bed afterward, I was physically exhausted but overwhelmed with gratitude for what the Lord was doing. My mind raced back to my encounter with the Lord on January 18, 2007 and how He spoke to me from John 17 about a new unity that would come across the earth. It was beginning to unfold right in front of me. Only the Lord could orchestrate a gathering of such diversity that could produce such stunning faith commitments to reach the world. All I could say was, "Thank You, Jesus," as I rolled over and closed my eyes.

After this Hong Kong event, the global call2all movement expanded rapidly. Country after country wanted their own congress or asked me to come and work with them on a national plan. In the following fourteen months, we did congresses in Eastern Europe, North America, New Zealand, the Middle East, Armenia, and Columbia. Each time, unengaged, unreached people groups were adopted. I could feel faith growing in the body of Christ and that the Great Commission really could be completed in a generation.

I communicated several times a week to the more than thirty thousand leaders who had been at a congress. They were hungry for the latest news on what God was doing. More congresses followed in quick succession: Malta, Indonesia, Western Europe, Paraguay, and the Philippines. One was also held in Los Angeles, California. While prepping for the Los Angeles event, I received a phone call from Matt Crouch, the son of Paul Crouch, the founder of Trinity Broadcasting Network. He had heard we were working on a congress not far from their Santa Ana studios and asked if he could interview me for a global TV show he was producing.

Matt and his camera crew arranged a room not far from LAX to do the interview. As I walked in, I could see the lights, cameras, and other equipment set up in a very professional manner. "Mark," Matt reached out his hand, "It's great to meet you. I've heard a lot about what you're doing around the world." Matt appeared to be very young, but he had an engaging personality, perfect for television.

"So what's our subject?" I asked. "We want you to explain what's going on in global missions. You're working with these thousands of leaders in the nations. We want to know your perspective."

Matt began the interview with a couple of questions about my family and then moved to the main subject. "Mark, tell us, from your perspective, what is happening in global missions?"

I began explaining the global picture. I talked about the 242 countries and territories, about how many people had been engaged and how many hadn't been, and about the important work of Bible translation.

About ten minutes into the interview, however, I realized that Matt and his crew were just staring at me and not asking any more questions. I stopped and said, "Is everything okay?"

Matt responded, "Mark, I don't even know what to ask you. We've never even heard these things before." Each of the camera team members in the room began nodding in agreement. "I realized, as you were answering my questions, I'm not qualified to do a program on global missions." I was impressed with his humility as he explained he had a limited view of what was going on across the world. "Mark, would you consider doing a show for TBN, a weekly program providing updates on the Great Commission?"

I wasn't ready for the question he was asking, and my mind began racing, thinking about the sort of commitment a show like that would take, what content might be used for the show, and who would produce it. "Matt, what would that entail?" I asked.

I could tell Matt didn't have all the answers but was willing to do whatever was necessary to get the show produced. "We would produce the show for you," he told me. "I would like my family to travel to some of your congresses. My boys can be the camera crew, and we can interview some of your delegates to get perspectives from other parts of the globe."

In the weeks that followed, we laid the plans for the program. One thing became clear: Matt didn't have anyone who knew enough about global missions to actually produce the show, and without the right producer, it wouldn't have the right feel. Matt generously offered to fund each broadcast if I could find my own producer.

I gave this challenge over to the Lord and began thinking about people I knew who could produce a show like the one we talked about. Jonathan Hall, affectionately known as "Jono," was leading the media team at the International House of Prayer in Kansas City. I knew he had some background with GOD TV in Africa. I called him, and we arranged a time to get together.

Meeting at my office at YWAM in Kansas City, I said, "Jono, Trinity Broadcasting wants me to do a weekly program on the Great Commission. I need someone to produce it. Are you interested?" Immediately, Jono began to share concepts with me on what the show could look like. It was obvious to me this was something the Lord had been preparing him for.

I began calling call2all partners to see if they would be able to provide me with video content from the nations of the world. They were willing and excited about getting this content out to a wider audience. In a matter of just a few weeks, we had content from major organizations coming in from around the world. This, along with the Crouch family filming fresh content at our congresses, would produce a dynamic weekly program unlike anything on the air.

We called the show call2all, named after the global movement. I asked Matt if we could announce the show on a live TBN broadcast. I would invite Loren Cunningham, Steve Douglass, and others to be on the main panel and have top Christian leaders from around the globe make up the audience. Matt loved the idea but had one suggestion: "Mark, I'd like to invite my dad, Paul, to join the panel. He and Loren go back many years."

The broadcast came together and was aired live before the LA call2all Congress. It was a dynamic show with powerful stories and insights into what God had been doing over the last half-century. The program was so popular, it was aired multiple times. Over the next three years, we produced thirty-three broadcasts of call2all. They were aired multiple times a week in more than one hundred countries.

God was changing the thinking of many people in the global body of Christ, helping His children understand the unfinished task of the Great Commission. Millions were coming together around common objectives. We were beginning to witness the power of a unified body under the leadership of Jesus. I kept thinking about Matthew 24:14, "And this gospel of the kingdom will be preached in the whole world as a testimony to all nations, and then the end will come."

Karen and I continue to serve the Lord with ever expanding opportunities across the globe. Our extended family continues to grow with more grandchildren and even a great grandchild!

Endnotes

[1] www.dictionary.com, s.v. "integrity."

Be a Faith Hero in Your Generation

The Bible is filled with stories of imperfect people accomplishing great things. In the list of genealogies and the heroes of faith there are murderers and prostitutes. These individuals made many mistakes, but are listed as faith heroes in their generations.

Finding your calling and achieving great things is not about perfection, it is about faith. The belief and trust in the unseen God that moves us to take great risks to obey his commands.

Entrepreneurs take calculated risks to make more money. Extreme sports athletes take risks for the adrenaline rush. We take faith risks because we trust an unseen God who has touched our lives. We do it to please him, we do it to bring other people into a relationship with the One we love. Any success in my life has been found by being willing to continually take risks of faith.

> *"Now faith is confidence in what we hope for and assurance about what we do not see."*
> Hebrews 11:1, NIV

Most people live by what they see, which leaves them controlled by circumstances. It is the opposite of Biblical faith. Often, God's callings make no sense to the natural, unrenewed mind. This is the way God designed things. He wants us to live by the Spirit, from the Spirit, and through the Spirit, living from the inside out.

Look at the list of faith heroes in Hebrews 11. By faith, Noah built an ark before it ever rained. By faith, Abraham and Sarah believed they would have the son of promise, even though they were physically unable to reproduce. By faith, Moses said no to wealth, power, and comfort to obey God. None of these things were rational according to normal thinking. If we are going to "conquer kingdoms", administer justice, take hold of the promises of God, see miracles, and find supernatural strength, we have to live by faith and take the corresponding risks.

Verses I often quote during times of prayer:

> [27] But God chose the foolish things of the world to shame the wise; God chose the weak things of the world to shame the strong. [28] God chose the lowly things of this world and the despised things—and the things that are not—to nullify the things that are, [29] so that no one may boast before him.
> 1 Corinthians 1:27-29, NIV

I understand He is the perfect, all-knowing Father that holds the universe together by His spoken word. I am a little boy offering Him my lunch so he can multiply it to feed thousands.

This book is entitled *Bold*. We are not bold because we trust our human strengths. We are bold because we serve a God who always keeps His word. Daniel prophetically wrote about a people who would know their God and do great exploits! You can be one of those people. Jesus said, "Open your eyes and look, the fields are ripe for harvest." All around us, are hurting and broken people. Go to them and bring good news. Go and heal the brokenhearted. Go and set the captives free.

When you finish reding this book, write down on a piece of paper the words "by faith" then after it, write your name, then write what God is calling you to do. Make the faith leap. Take the risk. Be bold!